The Himalayan Kingdoms

Bhutan, Sikkim, and Nepal

by PRADYUMNA P. KARAN

Associate Professor of Geography
University of Kentucky

and WILLIAM M. JENKINS, Jr.

Professor of Government
Western Kentucky State College

A SEARCHLIGHT ORIGINAL
under the general editorship of

GEORGE W. HOFFMAN
University of Texas

G. ETZEL PEARCY
United States
Department of State

D. VAN NOSTRAND COMPANY, INC.
PRINCETON, NEW JERSEY

TORONTO   LONDON

NEW YORK

D. VAN NOSTRAND COMPANY, INC.
120 Alexander St., Princeton, New Jersey
(*Principal Office*)
24 West 40 Street, New York 18, New York

D. VAN NOSTRAND COMPANY, LTD.
358, Kensington High Street, London, W.14, England

D. VAN NOSTRAND COMPANY (Canada), LTD.
25 Hollinger Road, Toronto 16, Canada

Published simultaneously in Canada by
D. VAN NOSTRAND COMPANY (Canada), LTD.

Preface

During the past decade a series of events has thrust the Himalayan kingdoms into world prominence. The brilliant conquests of Mount Everest, Annapurna, and Kanchenjunga captured the imagination of millions who have been hard put to locate Nepal, Sikkim, and Bhutan on a map. In 1959 the Tibetan revolt and the dramatic flight of the Dalai Lama from Lhasa focused the attention of the world upon this potentially critical area. More recently, the border clashes between China and India have dramatized the strategic location of the Himalayan kingdoms.

This book represents an attempt to evaluate the complex politico-geographic pattern of the Himalayan kingdoms. On a global dimension, consideration is given to the forces of democracy and Communism as they influence the three kingdoms. On a national scale, the special aspects of geographic location, physical environment, population, economic resources, and cultural heritage are studied in relation to their influence on political patterns.

During 1957 my field work in Nepal was supported by grants from the Population Council, Inc., New York, and the American Philosophical Society. During 1961-1962 I continued field studies in Sikkim and Bhutan on grants from the Association of American Geographers, the American Philosophical Society, and the Kentucky Research Foundation. I am immeasurably indebted to the University of Kentucky for granting me sabbatical leave during 1961-1962.

For permission to travel through the remote Himalayan regions, thanks are due to the respective governments. I acknowledge the assistance given by the Dewan of Sikkim; O. P. Mathur, Chief Engineer, Bhutan Roads; and the Indian Political Agent at Gangtok. I am indebted to G. V. Jani for help, enthusiasm, and good fellowship in the field. Without Khidu Tshering, my interpreter, the whole Himalayan journey would scarcely have been possible.

A special acknowledgement is due to Professor J. R. Schwendeman for his suggestions. C. D. Rai, a member of the Sikkim National Council, offered several suggestions on Chapter 3; Professors D. P. Varma (formerly of Trishuvana University, Katmandu), S. C. Chatterji (Vikram University, India), and C. Jha (Patna University, India) made many thoughtful criticisms of an earlier draft.

PRADYUMNA P. KARAN

3

Contents

List of Maps and Sketches

I   *The Himalayan Kingdoms*

"Among mountains, I am the Himalaya."
—Lord Krishna in *Bhagvad Gita*

Along the slopes of the Himalaya, between Communist-occupied Tibet and democratic India, lie the three little-known kingdoms of Bhutan, Sikkim, and Nepal. Completely land-locked and cut off from the rest of the world by mighty mountains and malarial forests, these small kingdoms remained a sealed book for a long time, territories whose rulers actively discouraged foreign visitors and alien ways. Until 1951 no more than a few hundred Westerners had seen the interior of these kingdoms, and only a few could locate any of the three on a world map.

Now this traditional isolation has changed. Tibetan revolt against Communism, the flight of the Dalai Lama to freedom in India, and the Chinese claim on Himalayan territories of India, Nepal, and Bhutan have attracted the attention of millions to this potentially critical world region. A major transformation is stirring in the remote highlands of these three kingdoms as their rulers attempt to change the middle-age feudalism of the Himalayan lands into the world of the twentieth century. The challenge of Communist aggression in the Himalaya has caused deep concern to the United States as well as to India and has brought these small countries into the forefront of ideologically induced tension between freedom and Communism. To meet that challenge demands change —basic reforms which must overcome internal resistance both from the landed aristocracy and from a people long accustomed to their lot, a people who have yet to develop a spokesman to articulate their needs and dimly-felt desires.

5

But Himalasia, to coin a regional term for the three kingdoms, faces tremendous problems in its surge into the modern world. Although Nepal, Sikkim, and Bhutan differ in area, population, natural resources, economic development, and structure of society, their politico-geographic problems are similar in many ways. Each kingdom must build a political organization. Administrative services necessary for a modern government must also be provided. Their economy, formerly adjusted to a feudalistic pattern of society, must be reorganized and developed. The social system, which in most cases had been outside the purview of feudal rulers, must be modernized and revitalized.

These Himalayan kingdoms, for the first time, face complex problems—without an adequate political and administrative organization, without essential skills and technical equipment, and also without a social preparation that could release the energies of the community to deal with the problem of transformation. The satisfactory solution to these problems is made more difficult by the rugged topography of the Himalayas. The nearly 75,000 square miles of these three Himalayan kingdoms contain some of the most forbidding terrain on the earth's surface. Environmental factors impose almost insuperable barriers to the unification of countries along nationalistic lines. In Himalasia is found one of nature's strongholds against man's modern political-administrative progress.

THE PHYSICAL LANDSCAPE

Millions of years ago the area now occupied by the Himalayan kingdoms was the site of the shallow Tethys Sea. During the tertiary period in the earth's geological history, powerful compressive forces folded and thrust marine deposits, which rose out of the waters in gigantic earth waves, and under the erosion of water and ice became a land of broken and irregular mountain masses. These crustal movements led to the development of a series of longitudinal valleys. Finally, in the post-tertiary age, also known as the Pleistocene, approximately one million years ago, further upheavals raised the central portion of the Himalayan range, together with the foothills, into a vast mountain system. In the follow-

THE HIMALAYAN KINGDOMS

1

ing milleniums, this was reduced by the forces of nature to form the present complex mountains and valleys of Bhutan, Sikkim, and Nepal.

From the standpoint of man's use of the complex mountain region, there are three salient features of this Himalayan geological structure. First, there is the great elevation of this mountain system, in particular its crystalline axis, whence the altitude and its train of consequences. Second, there are a variety of rocks, sometimes hard, sometimes soft. Their distribution in large masses has made possible the direct excavation of longitudinal valleys in soft rock and, indirectly, the deepening of others which are linked thereto; hence, the great contrast of high peaks and steep slopes. Lastly, there is the preponderance of length over breadth of this mountain system, which enabled man at an early date to penetrate a chain that could not be skirted. This final factor led to comparatively early settlement and cultivation despite the obstacles of altitude and topography.

The central portion of the great mountain mass is the most rugged. Here in majestic splendor, Mount Everest, conquered but defiant, holds court with spectacular Kanchenjunga, Makalu, Dhaulagiri, Gosainthan, and Annapurna—all, in their own right, kings among mountains. These peaks, with their snow-covered approaches, form a fantastic backdrop for the kingdoms of Bhutan, Sikkim, and Nepal on the frontier area between China and India. In the three kingdoms, "where gods are mountains," each peak symbolizes a god or deity who rules over the inhabitants of the land that it overshadows.

Physically this mountain mass is one of the few remaining isolated and relatively inaccessible areas in the world today. From a geographical standpoint there are three major lateral divisions, which to a great degree exhibit homogeneous regional characteristics: the Great Himalaya, the Inner Himalaya, and the foothills and bordering sub-Himalaya "Piedmont Plain," the latter locally called the *Terai* in Nepal and the *Duars* in Bhutan.

The first geographic division—the Great Himalaya—is adjacent to the plateau of Tibet. Here the peaks rise to 29,000 feet, and

PHYSICAL FEATURES

2

80 Miles
40   0   40

TIBET

⊙ LHASA

o Gyangtse

BHUTAN

SIKKIM

NEPAL

MT EVEREST
MAKALU
GAURISHANKAR
KANCHENJUNGA
GANGTOK
KATMANDU
DHAULAGIRI
ANNAPURNA
Pokhra
Jumla
GURLA MANDHATA

GREAT   HIMALAYA

INNER   HIMALAYA

SIWALIK   HILLS

TERAI

PLAIN

INNER

GREAT   HIMALAYA

HIMALAYA

DUARS

PLAIN

Thimbu
Paro
Punakha
Sankosh
Ama
Monos

Darjeeling
Biratnagar
Tista

Kanali
Rapti
Gandak
Bagmati
Kosi
Gauhati
Brahmaputra

INDIA

o Lucknow
o Patna
Ganges

EAST   PAKISTAN

N

GENERALIZED SECTION ACROSS THE HIMALAYAS

NORTH

Tibetan Plateau

Great Himalaya

SNOW

Inner Himalaya

Himalaya Foot Hills.

Terai

Ganges Valley

SOUTH

10,000'
5,000'

for much of the 700-mile northern border of the Himalayan kingdoms the mountains average more than 20,000 feet above sea level.
Although the formidable mountains rising out of the clouds have
challenged the development of large-scale trade and commerce
since ancient times, only limited trade flowed through the high
passes until recently. In fact, before the Communist occupation of
Tibet, the high Himalayan passes were among the few areas in the
world where free trade and travel persisted across international
frontiers. Caravans carried cloth, spices, and small manufactured
goods from India, Nepal, Sikkim, and Bhutan into Tibet, and
brought back salt, wool, and yak herds.

Physically, the Great Himalayan region is dissected into a series
of north-south mountain blocks by the Manas, Sankosh, Amo,
Tista, Kosi, Gandak, and Karnali river systems. The valleys of
these rivers and their tributaries are occupied by small clustered
settlements. Extremely cold winters and short growing seasons are
distinctive features. As a result, the farmers in the High Himalaya
are limited to one crop per year—potatoes, barley, and wheat being
most common.

The second region—the Inner Himalaya—is a complex area of
forest-covered ranges and intervening fertile valleys. While it is
not as forbidding as the Great Himalaya to the north, it has none-
theless served to further isolate the fertile valleys of the kingdoms
from the Gangetic plains of India and the plateau of Tibet. Except
for the major valley centers of Paro, Gangtok, Katmandu, and
Pokhra, the region in general is moderately populated.

Within the Inner Himalaya the intervening mountain ranges
tend to compartmentalize the populated valleys. Although the
natural drainage lines are largely north-south, the numerous gorges
and rugged mountains make travel in any direction difficult. Lateral
roadways and transport routes are almost nonexistent, and monu-
mental engineering feats are required to establish any east-west
surface transportation system linking the principal population
centers. Ropeways and a few "jeepable" roads have been built in
recent years, but the basic means of transporting goods and supplies
into the interior is by mule and often by "coolie back." Lacking

adequate means of easy communication, it is not uncommon for dwellers in neighboring Himalayan valleys to remain complete strangers.

The third region—the foothills and the sub-Himalayan Piedmont—comprise the Churia Hills, and the Terai and Duars plain. In general, the southern part of the Terai forms a densely cultivated belt along much of the Indo-Nepal border; the Duars lie south of Sikkim, but a small part extends within the borders of Bhutan. The northern Terai and Duars are negative areas which add to the isolation of the Inner Himalayan valleys. Here the rain forests and malarial swamps, inhabited by such wild animals as the tiger, elephant, rhinoceros, and wild boar, serve as barriers to easy access. The savanna, or elephant grass, which covers much of this region, grows to a height of 15 feet and is so dense that it even impedes the progress of the animals for which it is named. It makes human passage commensurately difficult.

HUMAN RESPONSES IN HIMALAYAN ENVIRONMENT

The environment imposes harsh living conditions on Himalayan peoples. The moderate relief and mild climate of the Inner Himalayan valleys (such as Katmandu Valley and Paro Valley) change to rigorous conditions that become increasingly restrictive at high altitudes. The harshness is most evident in the Great Himalayan region. Nowhere else in the world are the mountains so high. Nowhere else is there such a difference in level between the valley bottoms and the mountain summits. Nowhere else is there such a large mass of steep rocks rising to giddy heights, destitute of plant growth of any kind, unsuitable for any use whatsoever. The natural conditions, being extreme, restrict man's economic activity, especially agricultural, limiting farming possibilities and providing few opportunities for livelihood.

Altitude is obviously the most important environmental factor, causing rapid and profound physical changes in the Himalaya. The effects of altitude, however, are complicated by the site, exposure to the sun's rays, and relief, which enhance the regional or local differences in the Himalayan landscape.

The steep topography aggravates the effects of altitude. If the mountains were rounded with gentle, smooth slopes, the Himalayan peoples would have it much easier. But, in the Himalaya, the exact opposite occurs. The steep contours of the land influence the whole life of the inhabitants. Apart from the alluvial valley bottoms, there are few flat surfaces or even gentle slopes in the Himalaya. Most cultivation is done on sloping ground, where work is more strenuous and takes longer. The slope increases the effects of gravity on cultivated land, causing the soil to slide downward slowly; tillage speeds up this process by making the earth friable and depriving it of a plant cover for a fairly long time. Lastly, slopes cause an outstanding number of avalanches of great destructive power. Most avalanches occur outside the inhabited regions, but occasionally unexpected ones sweep away high-altitude settlements.

From the viewpoint of land utilization there are three zones— crops, forests, and alpine pastures. (See Figure 3.) The crop-growing zone or sector is very extensive, stretching up to about 10,000 to 11,000 feet; crop yields naturally diminish as the altitude rises. Except in a few areas, rice and corn are seldom cultivated beyond 6,000 feet. At higher levels they are replaced by wheat, barley, and potatoes. The hardy grains are often grown at altitudes as high as the permanently inhabited centers. It should be added that between 7,000 and 11,000 feet, soil and climatic conditions are seldom suitable for farming, and consequently the cultivated plots are small and crop yields are low.

Forests dominate land use in the Himalayan kingdoms. The forest zone can be subdivided into two sectors: (1) in the lower part are deciduous forests which have been greatly reduced by clearings, especially in Nepal and Sikkim; (2) above this sector are the conifers species with either persistent or deciduous leaves, better adapted to lower temperatures. The upper limit of the forest growth is related to relief, soil, and climate (particularly the winds); and the tree line is not clear-cut, often varying 500 to 1,000 feet, depending on exposure and the extent of shelter, from Nepal to Bhutan. Above the tree line, there is often shrubby vegetation composed mainly of prostrate mountain pines and rhododendrons mark-

LAND USE

EXPLANATION

Cultivated land

Forest and mountain pasture

Waste land (Alpine Tundra Glaciers, some isolated grazing and farming in mountain valleys)

ing the gradual transition from forest to the alpine pasture areas.

The high mountain pasture forms an essential part of the plant resources of the Himalayan kingdoms and has made possible livestock raising, without the need for preliminary forest clearance. It stretches from the forest zone to the perpetual snow-clad area, but the vegetation rapidly deteriorates as the altitude increases. The snow-clad areas, which cannot be utilized, constitute a considerable part of Nepal, Sikkim, and Bhutan.

Land use and resource development in the Himalayan kingdoms are dominated largely by physical forces beyond man's control.

HIMALAYAN PEOPLES AND CULTURAL PATTERNS

Over the centuries the narrow fertile valleys and the arable hillsides of the Himalaya have been peopled by hardy races who have adapted themselves to the rugged landforms and harsh climate. (See Figure 4.) Mongoloid tribes from Tibet, Indo-Aryan peoples from Northern India, and the Lepchas from Assam and Upper Burma have settled in the Himalayan valleys and developed separate cultural patterns. The compartmentalization of land has favored retention of tribal and cultural individualities. Even the transmigration of tribal groups within the area, particularly from Nepal into Sikkim and Bhutan, has led to little mingling among the peoples.

Regional characteristics of physical appearance may be distinguished in the population. People with dark skin and hair and brown eyes tend to predominate in the south, and fair (yellowish) coloring is characteristic of the more northerly area bordering Tibet. The people in the south are, in general, of larger stature than those in the north. The Mongoloid element is dominant in the Great Himalayan valleys, and Indo-Aryan is indigenous in the Terai and Duars. The Lepchas of Sikkim are both smaller in stature and different in coloring from the other population groups. In the Inner Himalayan valleys there has been some intermixing of the Mongolian and Indo-Aryan strains.

The major religions in the Himalayan kingdoms are Hinduism and Buddhism. The Hinduism practiced in the Himalayan coun-

POPULATION

T   I   B   E   T

⊙ LHASA

○ Gyangtse

NEPAL

Katmandu Valley

Bhatgaon

KATMANDU   Patan

0   MILES   3

BHUTAN

SIKKIM

Tista R.

Amo R.

Sankosh R.

Monas R.

Brahmaputra

Gauhati

I   N   D   I   A

Kosi R.

Bagmati R.

Gandak R.

○ Patna

E A S T   PAKISTAN

40   0   40   80 Miles

Urban Population is Represented by
Three Dimensional Spheres.
The Number of People in Towns is
Proportional to the Volume of the Sphere.

= 25,000
= 50,000
= 100,000

Each dot (·) Represents 2,000 Rural Inhabitants
localized by Thums.

tries, unlike that of Northern India, is of the Tantric cults.[1] Buddhism is dominant in the Himalayan valleys near the Tibetan border. Within the zone of Buddhism two regions can be distinguished on the basis of ritual and belief. The northernmost part is, in general, the area of Lamaistic Buddhism, very similar to that practiced in Tibet.[2] To the south, Buddhism is strongly influenced by Hinduism. In some areas, such as in the Katmandu Valley, there is a complex blending of the two, and many deities are worshipped by Hindu and Buddhists alike.

Lamaistic institutions and rituals play an important role in those areas that are marginal to Tibetan Buddhism, but customs and concepts alien to Buddhism, representing the remnants of animistic beliefs or older folk-religions, persist in the higher Himalayan regions. Prominent among these practices is the cult of mountain gods. High peaks are regarded as lords of certain geographical areas. Examples of this belief are the mystical role of Khumbila—god of the 19,297-foot Khumba peak—for the Sherpas, and Kanchenjunga for the people of Northern Sikkim.

Illiteracy is uniformly high in these countries, and there is a great diversity of dialects and languages. The existing multiplicity of dialects and languages has tended to enhance the cultural isolation of one region from another.

Generally speaking, the present pattern of settlement, involving three political units—Nepal, Sikkim, and Bhutan—reflects a highly diversified cultural landscape. Sizeable communities, such as the Katmandu Valley, the Tista Valley, and the Paro Valley, have sprung up around centers of population in the fertile valleys of the Inner Himalaya. These centers have served as core areas, or nuclei, for the development of the three kingdoms. Modern Nepal grew out of Gurkha conquests of the Central Himalaya; Bhutan and Sikkim grew out of the extension of authority and influence of the principal chiefs or governors over adjoining areas. The physical

[1] *Tantric* characterizes the system of doctrines and rites based on a class of religious texts known as *Tantras*, revelations of Siva.

[2] For the nature and origin of Tibetan Buddhism, refer to Snellgrove, D., *Buddhist Himalaya*, Bruno Cassirer, Ltd., Oxford, 1957.

difficulties involved in the development of lateral transportation patterns over the whole of the Himalaya encouraged the secluded growth of the Himalayan states. Historically, each political unit has built a limited circulatory pattern centered around its political core.

ISOLATION AND GEOSTRATEGIC LOCATION

For centuries the rulers of the Himalayan kingdoms kept out foreign influence by closely controlling traffic and virtually sealing the borders against foreigners, particularly Europeans. At the close of the Anglo-Nepali War (1814-1815), Nepal was forced to accept a British resident officer, but the country steadfastly refused to allow unrestricted travel, even by the resident officer. Only 13 years ago, after the Revolution of 1950, did Nepal open its door to foreigners. And only three years ago, in 1960, was the first American reporter, Paul Grimes of the *New York Times,* allowed to enter Bhutan.[3]

A recent article in the *National Geographic Magazine* describes Bhutan as "the world's last Shangri-La." [4] To the average American it gives an idea of a mysterious land of peace and contentment, and tends to hide the many geopolitical complexities of this strategic borderland between Communist Asia and the Indian subcontinent. Lacking accurate knowledge of the geography, peoples, and history of this region, many Americans visualize the Himalayan kingdoms as the home of a placid Buddhist population whose tempo of life has changed little over the centuries. To some extent this concept is true. However, the growth of power of the People's Republic of China and the Communist occupation of Tibet makes Himalasia a cold-war battleground between democracy and Communism. Chinese infiltration in the Himalaya has made millions painfully aware of the strategic location of the border states. Concern for their future independence, in the face of Communist aggression, has caused the Himalayan kingdoms to open their doors, cautiously, and look toward India and the Free World.

[3] See three illustrated articles and a picture report on Bhutan by Paul Grimes, correspondent of the *New York Times* in India, who visited Bhutan in June, 1960; *New York Times,* June 13, 14, 15, 1960.

[4] Doig, Desmond, "Bhutan: Mountain Kingdom Between Tibet and India." *National Geographic Magazine,* Vol. 120, September, 1961, pp. 384-415.

The events that have led the governments of the Himalayan kingdoms to lower age-old barriers serve to emphasize the significance of the area. Mountains are no longer sufficient guarantees against aggression. The mountain passes of Nepal, Sikkim, and Bhutan which have served as routes to the holy places of Tibet could be used by Chinese Communists to gain access to the fertile Himalayan valleys, the Gangetic plains, and indeed the whole of India.

POLITICO-GEOGRAPHIC ASPECTS

It is important to assess the major geopolitical aspects of the Himalayan kingdoms. Basically, these features are the result of interaction among three factors: Himalayan environment and cultural patterns; location between the two major Asian powers, China and India; and the changing character of the power pattern in Asian politics.

TERRITORIAL INTEGRITY OF THE HIMALAYAN KINGDOMS

One of the common politico-geographic problems of the Himalayan kingdoms is the lack of strong territorial organization resulting from the rugged nature of the terrain. The northern boundaries with Tibet are ill-defined, and for much of their length there are no accurate surveys. Only the Sikkimese border is demarcated satisfactorily, and this line comprises only a small portion of the total boundary. In the absence of clearly defined borders, China disputes the existing traditional boundary. In the past neither the Himalayan states nor China (nor Tibet) exercised effective political control over the frontier area in High Himalaya.

The inhabitants of the High Himalayan valleys are largely of Tibetan origin; they speak similar languages and share allegiance to Buddhist religious ideas and cultural traditions. The Chinese have continually tried to woo people of the frontier region who are many days away from central governments in Katmandu, Thimbu, and Gangtok.

The southern boundaries of the three kingdoms are clearly defined, but here strong centrifugal forces are at work. Were India as aggressively inclined as Communist China, loyalties of the Hindu people in the Terai and the Duars would be strongly attracted toward India. Currently there is considerable transmigration across the southern borders, and the line here shows characteristics found along the United States-Canada international border. People, currencies, goods, and ideas flow more freely across these boundaries than between the political core of the kingdoms and outlying districts.

The attraction of the northern and southern border regions of the Himalayan kingdoms toward Tibet, and to a lesser degree toward India, poses a potential threat to their territorial integrity.

DEMOGRAPHIC DIVERSITY AND SECTIONALISM

The existence of a state depends upon the will of its inhabitants. No such determination of adequate intensity is present among the peoples of the Himalayan kingdoms. One of the major problems of Nepal, Sikkim, and Bhutan lies in the lack of national consciousness or sense of national identity among the people. Tribal loyalties come first; national allegiance comes second, if at all. In the Himalayan kingdoms geography favors the retention of local identity. Elevation and climatic differences, along with varying soil capacities, are so pronounced as to induce variant cultural patterns within relatively small areas. Regional identity is aided by difficulties of communication which effectively block the exchange of ideas and normal acculturation expected in smaller countries.

A further problem related to population lies in the distribution pattern. The populations of the three Himalayan kingdoms are generally distributed along river valleys. Settlements are small and widely dispersed over much of the Himalayan area. Residents of one settlement feel that they have little in common with their neighboring settlement. Even in the major population centers the economic pattern tends to fragment the population rather than to make it cohesive. There is no labor movement of consequence, and difficulties of communication have so far prevented the tenant farmers from presenting a united front, although they share common problems and dissatisfactions. Lacking a common history and a common purpose, there is little to bind one Himalayan inhabitant to another in any movement of unity.

Superimposed upon, and in many ways basic to, these divisive forces is the problem of language. Problems rising from the likeness of languages along either side of the frontier are important, but more serious is the problem of the multiplicity of languages within the interior. Here the many dialects create a modern Babel, and the communication of ideas is all but prohibited by the lack of a common language. This multiplicity of languages imposes a serious obstacle to any attempt on the part of national governments to foster a feeling of national unity. As if this diversity of languages were not a sufficient handicap, illiteracy is almost universal, and the usual outpourings of governmental pamphlets, literature, and nationalistic material is of no avail. In the absence of widespread ownership of radios, the spread of information is a slow and tedious process of person-to-person contact.

There are two other cultural considerations: the state of health of the population and the state of technological ability. To develop a strong state requires a healthy, skilled population. The people of the Himalayan kingdoms are not skilled from the standpoint of modern technology. They are not healthy; infectious and dietary diseases are endemic to much of the area. In the south, particularly in Terai and Bhutan Duars, the incidence of malaria runs high. The disease is a tremendous factor in reducing efficiency of workers; it is a debilitating disease which cuts the effective output of the laborer and imposes a frightful burden upon individuals and the economic life of the nation. Steps have been taken to eradicate the insects which cause malaria, but they are far from complete. Dietary diseases such as beri-beri continue to plague the Himalayan nations. Like malaria, these diseases not only take a heavy toll of life, but cause serious economic consequences by reducing the capacity for physical work.

POLITICAL INTEGRITY AND STABILITY

The Himalayan states have been dependencies of one nation or another for much of their history. The tradition of government, on the basis of present boundaries, is very recent indeed. Nepal is a sovereign state at present; it exercises a full degree of control over its external affairs, but its economy is dependent upon India. Since 1955 Nepal has been a member of the United Nations, and it has been able to obtain economic aid from both the Free World and Communist nations. On the other hand, Sikkim and Bhutan are semi-independent kingdoms retaining a large measure of control over their internal administration, but they are guided by India in their foreign relations. Both Bhutan and Sikkim receive all necessary economic aid from India. The governments of these two kingdoms are acutely aware that a too sudden impact with the outside world might be disastrous. Looking to neighboring Nepal, now suffering from the ills of political immaturity and a bewildering surfeit of foreign aid, Bhutan and Sikkim have good reason to be cautious.

Reference has already been made to some of the more obvious problems of political control—the compartmentalism of the countries; the primacy of tribal loyalties; the difficulties of communication and the high rate of illiteracy, which make political cohesiveness nearly impossible; and above all, the almost universal absence of a sense of national unity and purpose. Throughout most of the region the national governments exercise *de jure,* but not *de facto,* control over their territories.

The basic task facing the Himalayan kingdoms is the necessity for creating centripetal forces of sufficient strength to overcome the physical and cultural pressures toward fragmentation. The "state-idea" [5] is extremely weak, in fact almost nonexistent. Unless an

[5] American political geographers define the concept of state-idea as the peculiar purpose or purposes for which a state stands that distinguish it from other states. Richard Hartshorne wrote, ". . . each state must seek to present to its people a specific purpose, or purposes, distinct from the purposes formulated in other states, in terms of which all classes of people in all the diverse areas of the region will identify themselves with the state that includes them within its organized area. This concept of a complex of specific purposes of each state has been called the "state-idea" by various writers following Ratzel, or by others the *raison d'etre,* or justification of the state." James, P. E., and C. F. Jones (editors), *American Geography: Inventory and Prospect,* Syracuse University Press, Syracuse, New York, 1954, p. 195.

effective sense of nationalism can be fostered in the region, the future of the small kingdoms as independent political entities is dim indeed.

A political nucleus is present in each of the kingdoms—Katmandu in Nepal, Gangtok in Sikkim, and Thimbu in Bhutan—but the influence of these core cities diminishes directly with the distance from their immediate environs. In none of the kingdoms does the core area perform services of sufficient national scope to command respect, obedience, and financial support from peripheral segments. There is no feeling of dependence upon the national government and little sense of national allegiance on the part of the average individual. As a matter of fact, with King Mahendra's suspension of the democratic experiment in Nepal, there is today but little participation in national affairs. And in this absence of a sense of indebtedness or obligation lies the chief political weakness.

PROSPECTS FOR VIABLE ECONOMIES

The economies of the three Himalayan kingdoms are fundamentally agricultural and depend upon subsistence farming based on a feudalistic pattern of land distribution. Mineral and other natural resources for industrialization are gravely limited. The only source of power is in the mighty streams that flow down the steep Himalayan mountain sides.

The agricultural use of the land has reached its maximum intensity with the present state of technology. In some areas, particularly in the Terai of Nepal, improved water control and the introduction of disease-resistant strains of grain could improve crop yields to some extent, but most of the land suitable for farming is already under cultivation.

The inhabitants possess some handicraft skills which might be employed in the establishment of manufacturers for foreign markets. Silver craftsmen and skilled weavers could be used to make luxury goods for other parts of the world. On a more realistic note, however, one must pessimistically observe that the possibilities of any sizeable economic development which would give the Himalayan kingdoms higher living standards seem remote indeed. The economic problems are not simple, and when added to the lack of technological skills and raw materials, illiteracy, disease, absence of national consciousness and paucity of effective governmental controls in both political and economic spheres, their solution becomes enormously difficult.

THE FLOW OF IDEAS AND GOODS

An essential politico-geographic feature of a state is the existence of a pattern of circulation that permits the free exchange of goods and ideas among the people within the territory. Through this circulation a national consciousness is cemented and a feeling of mutual inter-dependence between various areas of a country is furthered. In the Himalayan kingdoms this flow is a trickle. It is the lack of such a flow that contributes so much to the difficulties of establishing effective political control. Its absence furthers narrow regionalism and inhibits the development of a common national purpose. The limited road nets, weather-controlled air services, and the secluded nature of the mountain valleys lead to the conclusion that the problem of circulation is basic. Other obstacles to national integration will be much easier to solve with an increase in the ease and swiftness of communication.

THE POSSIBILITY OF UNION AND AN "ASIAN SWITZERLAND"

The Himalayan kingdoms could conceivably join in some kind of federation. Such a political and economic union would, of course, enhance the possibility of the establishment of a buffer "Asian Switzerland" between Communism and democracy in Asia. Certainly at first glance the similarity between the situation of Switzerland in Europe and the Himalayan countries in Asia is striking. From a physical standpoint, the two areas are somewhat alike. Each is a mountainous area, and in general terms it is possible to compare the Alps to the Himalayas. Switzerland's irregular borders have served to separate hostile European nations in the past, and her isolated position was but slightly less difficult to overcome than that of her Asian counterpart.

Like the Himalayan area, Switzerland possesses few natural resources, and only hydroelectric power is readily available as a source of energy. Its agricultural lands are limited, and its population of slightly less than five million people (approximately half that of the Himalayan kingdoms) occupies some 16,000 square miles, an area slightly more than one-fourth that of the Asian region.

In common with the Himalayan nations, Switzerland is composed of diverse linguistic groups, each having language and cultural ties with other nations along the country's borders. Other centrifugal forces are to be found in the diversity of religious groups and cultural patterns. The problem of establishing a responsible government has been complicated by the retention of some vestiges of medieval political units. The greater ease of communications and transportation is an important factor in maintaining Swiss unity.

The success of the Swiss experiment, however, is due to a variety of factors. First, the problem of maintaining territorial integrity was resolved, in part at least, by a policy of neutrality during the period when her territory was unattractive to her neighbors. During this period the country served as the site of many international conferences, and during periods of conflict Switzerland served as a diplomatic clearing house for belligerent nations. Gradually, the idea of Swiss neutrality received general acceptance. She remained neutral because it served the interest of other nations to have her do so.

A second reason, and perhaps one of the most important, is to be found in the attitude of the Swiss people. Sharing a common pride in the achievements of their forebears in attaining independence without outside help, the people developed a sense of unity over a period of six centuries. Further, the Swiss developed a viable economy and a high standard of living through the development of manufacturing skills, using the great hydroelectric resources of the country as an energy source. The people's unique craftsmanship, specialization in agriculture, and the establishment of international banking institutions maximized their potentiality. Finally, the encouragement of tourism resulted in a large inflow of foreign exchange.

Is the Swiss pattern possible for the Himalayan kingdoms? Admitting that development will differ in specific details, is there a possibility that the Himalayan kingdoms could assume the Swiss role? It must be noted from the foregoing analysis of the politico-geographic aspects that possibilities of such a role are remote. Even though Nepalese leaders have spoken in favor of such a role, the idea has received little encouragement from the other two kingdoms.

It is obvious that the three kingdoms are not a completely homogeneous whole. They share the strategic location, the rugged terrain, inaccessibility, and lack of natural resources, but beyond these common attributes there is little real similarity upon which to base a federation of the Swiss type. The contrast between Nepal and Bhutan, which lie within 100 miles of each other, is especially striking. Nepal, a completely sovereign state, has a comparatively distinct political history, a highly developed culture in the Katmandu Valley, and a stable government despite its thoroughly autocratic institutions. Semi-independent Bhutan, on the other hand, has enjoyed little stable government. Until the turn of this century, it suffered from internal strife. Each of the four penlops (governors) competed for an extension of power and influence. The ascendency to the post of Deb Raja, the temporal ruler, was decided by arms. The Dharma Raja, the spiritual ruler, the reincarnation of Buddha, was found as the need arose, among the highest families. Only since 1907, when the penlop of Tongsa District became the hereditary king, has there been a measure of political stability.

Bhutan still feels the crippling effect of internal wars fought during the nineteenth century. Much more than Nepal, it is a land of poverty and illiteracy. As a result of almost continuous civil wars, commercial activity has been limited, and agricultural practices are far more backward than those of the other Himalayan kingdoms.

Between Nepal and Bhutan is the tiny Indian protectorate of Sikkim with its fertile Tista basin. The base of the Sikkimese economy is much broader than that of its neighbors, including rich copper mining and cultivation of a variety of crops as well as livestock and dairy products for export. Despite Sikkim's small size, its developed productive capacity far exceeds that of larger Bhutan.

Its able government under the King, formerly under the protection of Great Britain, now of India, has permitted a gradual and orderly development of the resources of the country.

Certainly, the rulers of the three kingdoms will be loathe to surrender any of their personal power. If, however, the Himalayan nations are faced with the prospect of completely losing their present status under the dominion of foreign powers, particularly Communist China, they may achieve a certain degree of union. Such a union, coupled with improvements in communication (for example, the establishment of a radio system and a passable road network), may possibly lead to development of a Himalasia approaching an Asian Switzerland.

II

The Kingdom of Bhutan

"The world's last Shangri-la, now darkened by China's shadow. . . ."

—*National Geographic Magazine*

BHUTAN is the second largest kingdom in Himalasia, yet its 18,000-square-mile area is less than half that of the American state of Indiana. Geopolitically, the location of Bhutan between the Tibetan plateau and the Assam-Bengal plains of India gives the kingdom considerable strategic importance. The kingdom has a potentially adequate economic base, but its resources are underdeveloped and it remains the poorest among the Himalayan kingdoms. The economic core of the nation lies in the fertile Inner Himalayan valleys, which are separated from one another by a series of high and complex interconnecting ridges extending across the country from north to south. The remote and virtually inaccessible political nucleus is located in the Paro Valley in Inner Himalaya.

Since 1907 Bhutan has been ruled autocratically, but the feudalistic system of government is changing slowly, and the country seems to be evolving peacefully into a new democratic nation under India's guidance and protection.

Although Bhutan is "guided by the advice of the government of India in regard to its external relations," certain Bhutanese leaders are developing "sovereignty consciousness." The desire that Bhutan become a sovereign state has been expressed in the state's advisory council, and the issue of "guidance" by India has been the subject of heated discussion in the kingdom. Prime Minister Nehru has advised Bhutan against establishing diplomatic relations with foreign countries, and the king has accepted Nehru's advice. The present king, Jigme Dorji Wangchuk, a young man of 34, has made drastic changes in the system of government that may eventually lead to the establishment of a constitutional monarchy. Changing patterns in Bhutanese affairs are to be recognized in all aspects of the kingdom's politico-geographic development.

GEOGRAPHICAL STRUCTURE

Bhutan is best oriented by locating it with relation to the great chain of the Himalayas which arcs through the northern frontier of India. Occupying the eastern part of this mountain rampart, the small country has within its borders five passes leading into Tibet. The existence of these important avenues of approach to Lhasa has been a strong factor in influencing settlement and trade. Rivalry among tribal chiefs for the control of trade flowing through these passes has had significant impact on the historical development of Bhutan.

GREAT HIMALAYA

The northern part of Bhutan lies within the Great Himalaya, and the snow-capped ranges attain a height of more than 24,000 feet in some places. High valleys occur at elevations of 12,000 to 18,000 feet, running down from the great northern glaciers. The alpine pastures are used for grazing in the summer months only, when the hardy Bhutan cattle are taken up to 14,000 feet and the yaks to even higher elevations. The high alpine pastures form a comparatively broad base, from which the snow-capped mountains rise steeply.

North of the Great Himalaya are several "marginal" mountains of the Tibetan plateau. These marginal mountains are lower in elevation than the Great Himalaya; their summits attain a height of 19,000-20,000 feet at the most. They form the principal watershed between the rivers draining southwards and those flowing to the north. Further, these mountains separate the complicated structure of the Himalaya from the flat or undulating tableland of Tibet. Dry climate dominates the landscape north of the Great Himalaya, and in consequence there are no large valley glaciers in the Tibetan marginal mountains.

Until a few years ago the tempo of life continued in the Great Himalayan area much as it had for centuries. Long undisturbed in their ways, Bhutanese traders carried cloth, spices, and grains across the mountain passes into Tibet and brought back salt, wool, and sometimes herds of yaks. The tragic events in Tibet have badly shaken their tranquil isolation and the traditional uninhibited way of living. Now, thousands of Tibetan refugees swarm through the High Himalayan region to flee Communist-occupied Tibet.

INNER HIMALAYA

Spurs from the Great Himalaya radiate southward, forming watersheds between the principal rivers of Bhutan. Of these, the Black Mountain range, which forms the watershed between the Sankosh and Manas Rivers, divides Bhutan into two parts both administratively and ethnographically. To the east, in Tongsa Dzong, the people originally came from the hills of Assam, while to the west in Paro Dzong the population is predominantly Tibetan in origin.

The mountains provide climate controls that have a marked influence on temperature and precipitation. They act as barriers and intercept the moisture of the monsoon winds, with the result that heavy rains fall on the windward slopes while the descending air brings drier conditions on the leeward sides. Differences in elevation and the degree of exposure to monsoon winds encourage a variety of vegetation, ranging from dense forest on the rain-swept windward slopes to alpine vegetation on the highest peaks.

Central Bhutan lies in the Inner Himalaya and is comprised of several fertile valleys located at elevations varying from 5,000 to 9,000 feet, which, with their dividing ranges, extend southward for 40 miles. These valleys are healthful, relatively broad and flat, with moderate rainfall, and are fairly well populated and cultivated. Among them, the Paro (7,750 feet) and the Punakha (5,170 feet) valleys are the best known.

In the valley of the Paro River, in the midlands of Bhutan, the substantial houses cluster into villages or stand with white plastered walls and timbering amidst lush little fields of wheat or rice, peacefully guarded by their ranks of tattered prayer flags. The *dzong* (castle-monastery), built on an outcrop from the steep side of the valley, looms from afar, with its vertical series of prayer rooms and temples soaring above the outer courtyards with flattened roofs and richly painted windows. Paro *dzong* is temporarily the administrative center of the kingdom. It also frequently serves as venue for the sessions of the *Tsongdu* (the national assembly), attended by the ruler of Bhutan, His Highness, the Druk Gyalpo, and for the archery meet and ritual dances that characterize festivals in Bhutan.

The Inner Himalayan valleys have been formed by the erosive work of rivers; the valley bottom and the sloping hillsides on either side of the stream are rendered suitable for agricultural purposes by being cut into terraces. In Punakha Valley, which is least elevated among the Inner Himalayan valleys of Bhutan, a striking contrast is afforded by the sight of subtropical fruit trees such as mango and banana in the valley bottom, and the perennial snows of the arctic winter towering above them on the hoary mass of the Great Himalayas to the north.

DUARS PLAIN

The Duars of the Assam-Bengal plains reach northward into the borders of Bhutan for a depth of 8 to 10 miles. The mountains rise sharply and abruptly from the narrow Duars and are cut into deep gorges by rivers liable to sudden floods. The rainfall is excessive here, and hillsides are densely clothed with vegetation—forest as well as undergrowth. The entire Duars tract is unhealthy; the valleys are hot and steamy, while the higher ranges are cold, wet, and misty.

Bhutan Duars may be roughly divided into northern and southern portions. The southern portion is covered mostly with heavy savanna grass and bamboo jungle. In certain areas the savanna grassland has been cleared for rice cultivation. The northern portion of the Duars, or that immediately bordering on the hills, presents a rugged, irregular and sloping surface, marked by spurs which project into the plains from the more lofty mountains on the north. Deep valleys and open areas are, in some instances, found amongst these subordinate ranges, and the inhabitants of the Duars have established a number of small villages at the very foot of the mountains. The dense vegetation of the northern portion of the Duars swarms with elephants, deer, tigers, and other wild animals.

The narrow strip of Duars Plain contains access to the 18 strategic *Dooars* (doors or passes) through the Himalayan foothills leading into the mountainous central Bhutan. Eleven *Dooars* or passes are close to the northern border of West Bengal, and seven lie near the Assam border. From their sheltered defensive position in the mountains, the Bhutanese made frequent raids and incursions into Bengal and Assam through the *Dooars* in the eighteenth and nineteenth centuries.

DRAINAGE PATTERN

The entire mountainous territory of Bhutan is dissected by numerous rivers and their tributaries. The principal trade routes between central Bhutan and India follow the valleys of the main rivers. Almost all the large rivers of Bhutan (with the exception of the Manas and the Kuru) flow from the southern face of the Great Himalaya and, struggling through the narrow defiles at the foot of the mountains, emerge into the Duars, eventually to drain into the Brahmaputra. Through the Manas and Kuru River valleys lie two of the principal routes linking eastern Bhutan to Lhasa, the capital of Tibet.

The Mo Chu (or Punakha), flowing from the snow-capped mountains past Gasa Dzong, and the Pho Chu join in the Punakha Valley to form the Sankosh River. The imposing castle of Punkha stands on a strategic site commanding the Sankosh Valley. About 15 miles south of Punakha lies the celebrated castle of Wangdu Phodrang on the Sankosh. Near Wangdu Phodrang the mountains press more closely on the river, leaving but a narrow defile. Through this defile runs one of the important routes, and the command of the castle at Wangdu Phodrang has, in consequence, been regarded as one of the peculiar distinctions and responsibilities in Bhutanese history. The river Thimbu or Wong Chu flows past Thimbu, the capital of Bhutan, and runs southwards through the entire extent of the country, under the name Raidak, to Phunchholing (Phuntsholing) on the Indian border, in the Buxa Duar.

THE EVOLUTION OF THE BHUTANESE NATION

The historical origin of Bhutan is enveloped in obscurity. What knowledge exists concerning the origin of the kingdom is derived from old manuscripts found in Tibetan monasteries. During the past 500 years many Tibetan lamas from Kampa have visited Bhutan, settled there, and founded monasteries. Most of the larger monasteries and forts date back to 1500. Punakha was founded in 1527; Wangdu Phodrang was built in 1578.

The people whom the Tibetans found in Bhutan were Bhutia Tephoo, the tribe that originally settled the country.[1] The Tibetans did not expel these hardy natives who had come originally from Cooch Behar in India, but some of the natives moved down to the foothills and the Duars. Over three hundred years ago an influential traveling lama, Sheptoon La-Pha, became the king of Bhutan and acquired the title of Dharma Raja. It seems quite probable that Bhutan became a distinct political entity about this period.

La-Pha was succeeded by Doopgein Sheptoon, who consolidated Bhutan through the appointment of *penlops* (governors of territories) and *jungpens* (governors of forts) to administer the kingdom. Doopgein Sheptoon exercised both temporal and spiritual authority, but his successor considered that the two realms of authority were incompatible. The new Dharma Raja confined himself to the spiritual role and appointed a *dewan,* or minister, to exercise the temporal power. The dewan gradually became the Deb Raja (temporal ruler) of Bhutan. This institution of two supreme authorities—Dharma Raja for spiritual affairs, Deb Raja for temporal

---

[1] This section is based on Eden, Ashley, *Political Missions to Bootan,* Bengal Secretariat Office, Calcutta, 1865, p. 206. See also Pemberton, R. B. *Report on Bootan,* Bengal Military Orphan Press, Calcutta, 1839, pp. 716-722.

matters—existed until the death of the last Dharma Raja some thirty years ago. Succession to the spiritual office was dependent upon a verifiable reincarnation of the Dharma Raja. Customarily, the reincarnation satisfactorily established his identity as the promised spiritual head (Dharma Raja) by correctly recognizing the late Dharma Raja's cooking utensils placed before him along with similar articles belonging to other persons. When the last Dharma Raja died no reincarnation was found, and the practice and the office no longer exist.

No reliable records are available concerning the historical development of Bhutan during the seventeenth and eighteenth centuries. For much of the nineteenth century the country was plagued by a series of civil wars as the penlops of the various territories contended for power and influence. The office of Deb Raja, in theory filled by election by a council composed of penlops and jungpens, was in practice held by the strongest of the governors, usually either the Paro penlop or the Tongsa penlop. Similarly, the penlops, who were to be appointed by the Deb Raja, actually fought their way into office.

The jungpens were selected by the penlops from among their followers. As a consequence, every change of penlops was followed by a change of jungpens subordinate to them. The superceded officials generally established themselves near the fort to await an opportunity to return to power. For more than two centuries there was a continuous series of skirmishes and intrigues throughout the land.

Until the turn of the twentieth century, Bhutan, although a political entity, had no central government. It was split into a number of smaller divisions along feudalistic lines; every seat of power was subject to a continuous contest between unscrupulous chiefs who aspired to dominion. However, in 1907, the penlop of Tongsa, the most powerful of the penlops for many years, became the hereditary king (Gyalpo). The present king, Jigme Dorji Wangchuk, (the "Fearless Mighty One"), is the third in this line; his grandfather, with the help of the British, established himself as sole ruler at the beginning of the century. In the 11 years during which he has been king, Wangchuk has been devising means of advancing his country from the sixteenth into the twentieth century with speed, but with the least possible pain. He has planted seeds of social and economic change which have already begun to blossom. The new roads being driven into Bhutan from the plains of India are the symbol of rapid change initiated by the king, who enjoys great personal popularity and moves among his people with affectionate freedom. His wife, Queen Ashi Kesang (meaning "Good Destiny"), niece of the maharaja of Sikkim and younger daughter of the late Bhutanese prime minister, Raja Dorji, attended school in England before marrying King Jigme Wangchuk in 1953. Bhutanese who are aware of the kingdom's internal situation take the queen's name to be a good omen for the future of this inaccessible country. They hope that the Royal couple, with their European education, will carry out sorely needed reforms; for only in this way will "The Forbidden Kingdom" of Bhutan be able to preserve its autonomy amidst the dark shadow cast by Communist China around its northern border.

During the last decade, Druk Gyalpo has introduced many social reforms to liberate his medieval subjects from their past. He freed about 5,000 slaves, giving them a choice of continuing with their masters as paid servants or accepting land from the government and setting up as farmers. He ended the traditional Bhutanese custom of prostration in the king's presence and in that of his senior officers. He has set up schools in which the medium of instruction is Hindi, since Bhutanese must go to India for higher education. With an energetic campaign he has almost completely stamped out the venereal diseases that were once endemic in Bhutan, and he has instituted the *Tsongdu* (national assembly) to serve as a medium between ruler and people. Despite these efforts, Bhutan has a long way to go for national integration. At present it lacks a national consciousness; people living in isolated valleys think of themselves primarily as Bhutias or Nepalese rather than Bhutanese.

BHUTAN'S BOUNDARIES WITH INDIA
AND CHINA

Bhutan has both natural and arbitrary boundaries. In the north the Tibet-Bhutan boundary is undefined. Here the traditional boundary follows the crest of the Great Himalayan range, which also forms the watershed for the most part. However, China does not recognize this customary watershed boundary as valid. The Chinese claim about 300 square miles of northeastern Bhutan and a substantial area to the north of Punakha, the former Bhutanese capital.[2] This territorial claim on Bhutan is based mainly on ethnic similarity with Tibet. There has been no reported incursion of Chinese troops along the Bhutanese border, but Tibetan trade, particularly the export of Bhutan's surplus rice to Tibet, has completely stopped as a result of the boundary dispute. This cessation of trade has caused great economic distress to the Bhutanese farmers. The Chinese Communists in Tibet were irked by the cessation of trade with Bhutan, and during 1960 there were reports in Paro Valley of menacing speeches made in Tibet about the ultimate need to "liberate" Bhutan. Until now China has been conciliatory in its references to Bhutan, stating that there are no grounds for disagreement with that country. Bhutan, however, acting through India, as by treaty it must, has complained about Chinese maps which show parts of her territory within China.

In the Bhutan Himalaya, people have settled up to the water-parting of the rivers since ancient times, and the watershed range has served to separate the spheres of influence of the Bhutanese principality from that of the southern Tibetan tribes. The watershed range (the crest of the Great Himalaya) has thus evolved in Bhutan as the frontier with Tibet through settlement, custom, and tradition. The use of the watershed range as the boundary in the Himalaya has considerable support in history. Discussing Himalayan boundaries, the preface to the report of the Pamir Boundary Commission (1895) states that "geographically, politically, and ethnographically,

[2] *The Statesman,* Calcutta, March 17, 1960.

watersheds . . . are the only true and stable boundaries in these regions. . . . The possession up to the headwaters of each system by one people constitutes the only frontier that has survived the lapse of time." [3]

Bhutan's boundary with India lies close to the Himalayan foothills in the Duars plain. The present boundary line has evolved as a result of the British annexation of a major portion of Bhutan Duars adjoining Assam and Bengal between 1841 and 1864. This territorial loss deprived Bhutan of potentially productive agricultural land which could have substantially augmented the economic base of the nation.

In 1774, following the Bhutanese invasion of British-protected Cooch Behar State in India, the British Indian government signed a peace treaty on the basis of the return of each country to the boundary in the Bengal Duars as it existed before the Cooch Behar invasion. With the extension of British rule in Assam, following the first Burmese War (1825-1826), the British Indian government confirmed the boundary agreement between the Assamese and Bhutanese. According to this agreement, the British occupied the Durrang Duars in Assam from July to November of each year. During the remainder of the year it was to be occupied by the Bhutanese, who paid annual tribute in kind. The sale price of the tribute never equalled the value at which it was appraised by Bhutan. As each year's tribute fell short of the fixed amount, arrears developed. British demands for the liquidation of the growing indebtedness were met by evasion and a series of plunders of Assam territories near the border between the years 1828 and 1839. These events were followed by the annexation of the Bhutan Duars adjoining the province of Assam in 1841, and the present Assam-Bhutan border dates from that time.

Likewise, between 1837 and 1864, continued raids by the Bhutanese on the Bengal Duars led to the permanent annexation of the Duar territory adjoining Bengal in 1864. In 1865, under a treaty signed at Sinchula Pass near the Indian border, Bhutan assented to the

[3] *Report on the Proceedings of the Pamir Boundary Commission,* Government of India, Calcutta, 1897.

formal cession of the Duars to British India in return for an annual subsidy to be paid from the revenues of the ceded territory. The area of Bhutan ceded to India in the two annexations comprises the 18 Duars, a narrow strip of territory at the foot of the hills, averaging 22 miles in width and 215 miles in length. These annexations fixed the present southern boundary of Bhutan.

Bhutan's advisory council has resented the way in which the Bhutan-India border is shown on Indian maps. The Bhutanese leaders want the border to be shown clearly as an international boundary. Also, in the advisory council of the Maharaja, there have been stirrings of the kingdom's desire to develop as a sovereign state in the fullest sense with foreign relations of its own. But without well-developed communications, such relations would be a fantasy.

HUMAN FACTORS

With its estimated population of 850,000, Bhutan is the second most populous Himalayan kingdom after Nepal.[4] However, its density of population—47 persons per square mile—is the lowest of the three kingdoms. The most sparsely populated sections are the broad Great Himalayan region and the unhealthy malarial foothills bordering the Duars. Adverse physical conditions in both these areas limit most of the population to the Inner Himalaya valleys of central Bhutan. Not only is the country more sparsely populated in comparison to the other kingdoms, but its population is increasing at a lesser rate. In contrast to Nepal and Sikkim, the villages are generally small and widely separated. The unevenness of population distribution makes political cohesiveness difficult.

Bhutan's population is entirely rural. The kingdom has no towns, no banks, no shops worthy of the name. Thimbu, the new capital under construction with Indian aid, is now a mere cluster of houses around the *dzong,* a fortress built in the architectural style of the

[4] The population figure of 850,000 (1963) is the author's estimate based on field study of the demography of the kingdom. It is supported by the examination of settlement pattern on the new large-scale topographic maps and air photographs. In almost all publications, during the last fifteen years, Bhutan's population is given as about 700,000.

Kingdom of BHUTAN

A choiten gate in Wangdu Podhrang in central Bhutan

Bhutanese Minstrel

The most famous of
Bhutan's bridges at
Wangdu Podhrang

Thimbu Dzong — Thimbu is new capital

Roger

potala, or palace of the Dalai Lama, at Lhasa. Likewise, Paro, the temporary capital, is still no more than a *dzong* and collection of houses. Electric lights, drainage, and similar modern innovations are still unknown in faraway Paro and Thimbu. Paro's only modern installation is a small radio transmitter, which maintains contact with the Bhutan House in Kalimpong, India.

Despite centuries of living together, different ethnic groups retain their distinguishing characteristics, and distinct types are to be found in different regions. Those living in the western half of the kingdom, to the west of the Black Mountain Range, are for the most part of Tibetan origin, having settled in the country centuries ago. In Eastern Bhutan the bulk of the population is of non-Tibetan stock, similar to the people of the adjoining North East Frontier area of Assam. Both population groups are Buddhist, but those of eastern Bhutan are less strict in their observance of religious customs, and there are fewer monasteries and lamas.

In addition to these groups, there are Nepali-Hindu settlers who have moved along the foothills and form a considerable community along the whole length of southern Bhutan where the outer hills join the Duars plain of India. Although this Hindu element provides a needed settlement of the lower hills, it also adds to the political discontent and instability.

In Bhutan, as in Sikkim, the dominant religion is an offshoot of Buddhism introduced by lamas from Tibet. Since Buddhism is the state religion, lamas are supported at state expense. Bhutan supports about 4,000 lamas who are attached to eight monasteries. More than a quarter of the state revenue is spent on monasteries. Lately, attempts have been made by the king to reduce their number by leaving the vacancies caused by death unfilled.

Illiteracy in Bhutan is universal; most of the population can neither read nor write. In the Paro Valley and border towns where social strides are most marked, a small, literate class is taking root. Political and cultural alertness stamp this group as one of the greatest sources of potential strength in Bhutan.

In the last two years nearly 70 government schools teaching Bhutanese, Hindi, and English have been opened in various parts of the mountain kingdom. A peculiar system prevails in the schools. They are largely residential, and parents supply the rations for their children and do the cooking by turns.

Differences in language, religion, and ethnic origin have their effect on the political life of this tiny kingdom. The people generally think of themselves in terms of their respective tribes or ethnic origin. The principal minority element is the Nepali settlers of southern Bhutan, who constitute an estimated 25 per cent of the population. In the Nepali-settled areas along the southern fringe of the kingdom there is an acute shortage of land, and the Nepalese are banned from living in the central highlands. As a result, there exists a degree of resentment against the Bhutanese rulers. In practice Nepalese are second-class citizens, despite the stated desire of the government to integrate them with the highland Bhutanese. Discrimination shown against them by the government constitutes a serious political weakness of Bhutan.

The king has endeavored to modernize the social structure of Bhutan. For example, besides declaring serfdom illegal, he has abolished polyandry and restricted polygamy to a maximum of three wives per man. But before taking a new wife, the man must obtain the permission of his first wife, who is free to seek a divorce and maintenance for life from the husband. The age for marriage has been raised to 16 for women and 21 for men. On marriage the bride does not necessarily leave her home; it all depends on the strength of the two families as an agricultural labor force. The groom comes over if the bride's family's labor needs are greater. If both families have ample labor, then the couple may stake out their own plot of land and home.

ECONOMIC FACTORS

Despite the small size of Bhutan's total population, limitation of resources in the kingdom has generated population pressures, especially in the intensively cultivated Inner Himalayan valleys. Although precise figures are not available, a land-use[5] survey indicates that the total amount of land available for agriculture is only a

[5] A reconnaissance land-use survey carried out by P. P. Karan in 1961-1962.

fraction of the total area of the country. Adverse climate, poor soil, and steep slopes have made it necessary to leave a large land area in forest growth, alpine meadows, and grasslands. Of the three major regions of Bhutan, the relatively low, well-watered, and fertile valleys of Inner Himalaya have the largest percentage of cultivated land, and it is here that agriculture is most intensively developed. The Bhutanese cultivator lays out land in a series of terraces; each terrace is divided and supported with a stone embankment, and every field is carefully fenced with pine branches. A nearly complete system of irrigation is practiced through the cultivated part of the valleys. Water is usually brought from a great distance through stone aqueducts.

Because of the great variation of elevation and climate there is scarcely any crop that may not be produced with facility in Bhutan. Within a radius of a few miles, and often within the boundaries of a single village, agricultural terraces are to be found at heights varying from 4,000 to 9,000 feet. Rice and buckwheat grow well up to an elevation of 4,000 feet. Barley alternates with rice from this altitude to about 8,000 feet; wheat grows at altitudes up to 9,000 feet. Centuries of cultivation of rice without manuring encourages soil erosion along the rugged slopes and tends to deplete the fertility of the soil. It is doubtful whether Bhutanese farmers will introduce the progressive changes in agriculture suggested by Indian experts, which include less dependence upon rice as a major food crop, because dietary habits are as difficult to alter as the farming practices that have followed well-established customs for centuries. Yet, unwise use of limited land leads to lower agricultural production and a shortage of food supplies, the fundamental cause for the creation of political unrest.

In recent times several land reforms have been introduced.[6] For instance, the government has restricted individual ownership of land to 30 acres. Even the maharaja owns only 30 acres. The system of land taxation has been modernized; the payment of tax in kind

[6] For details see Moorthy, K. K., "Bhutan—The Economic Scene," *Far Eastern Economic Review,* Vol. 31, February 23, 1961, p. 333.

has been replaced in some regions by cash payments on a trial basis.

Pastoral activities are common to all regions in Bhutan. The interesting practice of driving cattle up the mountainsides in the spring and down again in the autumn (called "transhumance") enables the Bhutanese to utilize pastures on the High Himalayan slopes during the warm season when they are free from snow. Yaks, as well as sheep and goats, are employed by the Bhutanese as beasts of burden. Salt, the commodity generally transported in this manner, is carefully sewn up in small canvas bags which are slung over the backs of animals.

Although a large part of Bhutan is covered by forests, lumbering is not developed because of the inaccessibility of the timber. Bhutan has no proved mineral deposits of significance, and mineral production is of little importance to the economic development of the country. There is a proposal to mine coal deposits in southeast Bhutan and supply coal to the tea gardens of Assam. Bhutan plans a geological survey; the organization will initially be manned by Indians.

With the sealing of the Tibetan border, Bhutan's trade is now limited to India. Under the 1949 treaty there is free trade between India and Bhutan, and India provides facilities for the carriage, by land and water, of Bhutan produce. Further, India has given Bhutan the right to use the Indian forest roads along the border area. Bhutan is free to import, through India, whatever arms, ammunition, and machinery are needed for the defense and welfare of the kingdom.

Bhutan uses Indian currency except for two token Bhutanese coins. However, money means little to most Bhutanese because barter is widespread in the kingdom. As a result of the barter economy, the *dzongs,* which serve as revenue collection centers in Bhutan, are full of homespun cloth, rice, wheat, butter, and dried yak meat.

All of Bhutan's foreign-exchange needs for development purposes are met by the Reserve Bank of India. The maharaja has a personal import license of 500,000 rupees (approximately U.S. $100,000) a year. There is no ceiling on the Government's import license. The Reserve Bank of India makes exchange available for the Bhutanese government for the asking. However, the total imports have been around 300,000 Rupees (approximately $60,000). Even the maharaja's yearly personal license is not being fully utilized. The fact is that without power supply or roads for wheeled traffic, there are not many things on which Bhutan can spend foreign exchange.

JALDHAKA POWER PROJECT

In September, 1961, India and Bhutan signed a pact to harness the River Jaldhaka for hydroelectric power. Rising in Sikkim, the Jaldhaka River runs along the border of Bhutan and India for 12 miles. The project involves construction of a diversion weir on the border, partly in Bhutan, but mainly in West Bengal. From the weir water will be brought to the power house through a tunnel 2½ miles long. Near the site of the power house, thousands of workers are already busy building roads, staff quarters, and the powerhouse buildings. The project will generate 18,000 kilowatts of power; and Bhutan will receive a free supply of 250 kilowatts. Further, India will pay a royalty of eight Rupees (approximately $1.60) per kilowatt annually. In addition to bringing much benefit to the northern areas and tea gardens of West Bengal, the Jaldhaka hydroelectric project will be a great boon to southwestern Bhutan, which has no coal and oil supplies and experiences considerable transport difficulty.[7]

ECONOMIC AID AND DEVELOPMENT PLAN

In order to speed its economic progress, Bhutan, which so far has received only Indian aid, is now seeking additional assistance from western countries. The government is negotiating with a Swedish company for technical assistance in developing a paper industry based on the rich pine forests of southern Bhutan. If this project materializes, it will be the first industrial enterprise in Bhutan. The

[7] Moorthy, K. K., "Bhutan: Pact on Power Project," *Far Eastern Economic Review,* Vol. 34, October 5, 1961, pp. 7-9.

decision to welcome western experts, though only where it is felt they can contribute to economic development, is a sharp departure from Bhutan's traditional policy. India does not favor Bhutan's direct negotiation with foreign governments for aid, but negotiations with private foreign enterprise have not met with Indian objection.

In July, 1961, Bhutan announced a five-year development plan which aims at increasing the kingdom's internal revenues and eventually creating a self-reliant economy. This $36,750,000 (172,-000,000 Rupees) development plan, financed by India, places a major emphasis on road and transport development. India is eager to bring Bhutanese, who have ethnic ties with Tibetans, closer to her by improving communications. At the same time the development of transport would help build defenses in Bhutan to combat possible aggression by the Chinese Communists.

Scarcity of labor is one of the main problems that Bhutan has to face in implementing her development plan. The kingdom has an estimated population of 850,000, and most of the people are already employed in agriculture and other vocations. Where keeping foreigners out of Bhutan was once of prime importance to the government, it has now become essential to recruit outside the country hundreds of skilled personnel to serve as technical experts, advisers, engineers, doctors, and teachers in the new development projects. Bhutan is recruiting from India administrative officials to head its new department of agriculture, health and forest, and an economist to serve as financial adviser to the kingdom. A former chief secretary of Sikkim, T. D. Densapa, has been appointed director-general of development. It is estimated that by 1963 Bhutan will need a labor force of nearly 30,000 to work on the roads, the administrative buildings, and a 50-bed hospital and other construction projects. About 25,000 Bhutanese are already working on various construction projects, and the remaining labor force of 5,000 will have to be recruited in India, in addition to hundreds of skilled Indian personnel. The Bhutanese government does not find the Tibetan refugees, numbering about 4,000, to be competent workers on road construction and other building projects.

TRANSPORT DEVELOPMENT

The economic development of Bhutan has long been handicapped by physical barriers which have reduced the accessibility of various areas—and of the kingdom itself—to people and to ideas. Movement, essential to the establishment and maintenance of political and economic organization, is poor. As a result, it is difficult to weld the isolated groups of people into a unified, viable state.

Nature gave Bhutan strong doors, and they are now being opened with difficulty. Until 1961, to enter this Himalayan kingdom the traveler trekked for days on foot and on muleback, striking from the mild plains of Northwest Bengal into a forbidding maze of thickly forested sharp ridges alive with leeches. For instance, the track followed by travelers going to Paro climbs the ridges in tight zig-zags so steep that mules pause every few yards to pant. Often the trail crosses high passes broken with rocks and mud pools that have even the mules stumbling; for a distance the route follows the ridge-top until it is time to descend to the warmth of the river bed, and then the whole exhausting process begins again over the next ridge.

To Paro, the nearest inhabited valley in west central Bhutan, it is six days' hard trekking from the Indian border. On the way the traveler sees few signs of human activity. Now and again a mule train will be drawn against the side of the ridge to let his party pass—or, perhaps, if the leading mule carries the banner of one of the members of the royal family of Bhutan, he will yield the right of way. On the far side of a valley there may be glimpses of a patch of terraced fields and a scattering of huts bristling with Buddhist prayer flags.

During 1960-1962 there has been new activity—signs of change in Bhutan—along the mountain track leading to Paro. Tents in the forest clearings, Indian survey crews, and small parties using picks and axes to clear a narrow pathway marked the preliminaries to construction of a new road that, since 1962, has carried jeeps to Paro in one day's journey. In late 1961 the new road had already reached out 100 miles into the Himalaya from Phunchholing

(Phuntsholing), a village of Bhutan just south of the ranges that elsewhere make the border with India.

From the beginning of the century (when the idea was first broached by the British authorities) until 1959, the rulers of Bhutan had refused to allow a road to be built. Topography had closed their little country to the outside world, and they preferred to bolt these natural barriers by discouraging all travelers. Behind them Bhutan could follow its own ways undisturbed, its rulers autocratic and at times despotic, its people paying their taxes to their governors and the monasteries, trading a little with Tibet and India, but insulated effectively from all society other than their own.

Suddenly, in 1960, the government of Bhutan changed its policy of isolation. Indian assistance to build roads was sought. Three north-south roads from the Indian border to central Bhutan are being built in addition to the Phunchholing-Paro Highway. A lateral east-west road connecting the north-south highways has been planned across central Bhutan. Aware of the military vulnerability of Bhutan if Chinese Communist aggression spreads, India is lending money, engineers, and surveyors for the construction of nearly 800 miles of new roads. Bhutan is providing a gigantic labor force of 25,000 men and women working in rotation and recruited under a new law making work on the national highways compulsory. Each family in a district is required to provide one laborer for road construction, with the option of replacing him or her with another after three weeks or a month. The government hopes to complete the ambitious plan of road building by 1966.

The principal highway of the country, which runs 120 miles from Phunchholing on the border with India to Paro (7,200 feet), the temporary capital, was completed in the spring of 1962. With the completion of this road, Paro saw its first motor vehicles in 1962. More significant, Bhutan's centuries-old seclusion from the outside world was finally ended. About 22 miles of the new road is threatened by the rampaging of wild elephants. Bears, reptiles, and leeches are a further menace on the southern part of the highway. An offshoot from the Phunchholing-Paro highway will lead to Thimbu, the new permanent capital. The completion of this first of five projected automobile highways has reduced the travel time between Paro and the Indian frontier from the previous six days by mule and foot to ten hours by jeep.

The proposed east-west road in Central Bhutan will run across the high range of the Black Mountain via the 11,055-foot Pele Pass, about 20 miles northeast of Wangdu Phodrang. West of the Pele Pass, the construction of roads is in the hands of the Bhutan Engineering Service, comprised largely of Indians in the service of the Bhutan government. Road construction east of the pass is the responsibility of the Border Road Development Board, an Indian combine of civil and military engineers. Under both are young Bhutanese in training.[8] If there is one dominant reason for the change in Bhutan's policy of seclusion and its sudden scramble toward physical access with the modern world, it would seem to lie in Chinese actions in Tibet. For centuries there had been trade between Tibet and Bhutan, Bhutanese rice selling at high prices in Tibet and bringing back its value in salt, wool, or Chinese silver dollars. Lately the Chinese Communists in Tibet have forced the acceptance of paper currency, worthless in Bhutan, and in other ways harassed traders. Perhaps more important, the traders had begun to bring back to Bhutan, along with their loaded mule packs, "mental cargoes of propaganda." In 1959, afraid of the spread of Communist propaganda, the government of Bhutan stopped all trade with Tibet. Bhutan recalled its trade representative in Lhasa in 1960. Now the *cordon sanitaire* between Bhutan and Tibet is breached only by a trickle of refugees.

With this embargo the price of rice in Phari (the trading town in Tibet to which the mule trains from Bhutan used to go) has risen sharply, while in Bhutan it has fallen by half, and there are complaints that the government has not kept its promise to buy the rice that can no longer be sold in Tibet. In the national assembly members complained in May, 1960, of the government's failure to provide an alternative market for rice and of the poorer quality of salt they now had to take from India. To all these complaints, the reply of

[8] Doig, Desmond, "Door to Forbidden Kingdom Opened," *The Statesman,* Calcutta, February 16, 1962.

the government—which treats this assembly as no more than a sounding board—amounted to "wait for the road." Now, in 1962, the Bhutanese farmers have already started transporting to West Bengal by the new road the surplus rice that food-short Tibet once bought and that India needs, but that until recently could not be economically shipped.

The decision to cut off the country from all exchange with Tibet required opening it to the south, and in this enterprise Bhutan will continue to receive the eager cooperation of India. Strategically, Bhutan is a disturbing gap in India's eastern defense line, and the roads now being built will enable India to move troops into that country if it is attacked. Politically, too, India has regarded a closed Bhutan as an invitation to subversion by progressive but potentially hostile forces, and it is ready to cooperate with economic and technical assistance in Bhutan's belated entry into the twentieth century. But India wishes to regulate the pace herself, whereas the rulers of Bhutan think themselves best fitted to judge their country's capacities.

CHANGING BHUTAN

The task of transforming Bhutan from medieval age to modern times has been well begun by the king and his government, but it has barely gained momentum. The people, living mostly in the valleys that run north and south between the spurs of the Himalaya, have been little touched by change. Their self-sufficient villages, tall houses, and castle-monasteries give an impression of a small fairy-tale land—contented, uncluttered, and untouched. It is not so much an economic gap that a visitor crosses to enter a Bhutanese house as a gap in time. By Indian standards, there is adequate food to eat in these families, large as they are now that infant mortality has been reduced. Their rooms are high and spacious. There is generally some richness about the altar in the prayer room, which is often as large as the living area. But all the rooms are dirty, buzzing with flies, and blackened with smoke (there are no chimneys).

In sickness the people call on the witch doctor, the *pau,* or the lamas. Black magic is a part of Bhutanese life. Ghosts, witches, and clawing spirits are so familiar that often valleys and settlements are named after them. (For instance, Bumthang, an important settlement in Central Bhutan, means "the Plain of Spirits.") To avert illness and other misfortunes the Bhutanese wear their amulets and have their dusty scrolls hung from the rafters, sending up the prayers as they rustle dryly in the draft. Their religion is touched with the relics of *bon,* the cult of devil worship that existed in Bhutan before the word of Buddha came.

The Bhutanese are obviously a happy people, characterized by dancing children and almost child-like adults who merrily hiss and whistle at the villainous masked monsters of elaborate lama dances. One is forced to wonder what persuaded the rulers of this little country to open it to all the turbulence of change? The explanation lies in the recent happenings in Tibet. Bhutan, possibly first on the list of Chinese expansionist aims, must change in order to preserve her territorial integrity. Change is ineluctable, and the Bhutanese have chosen not to wait for it to be forced upon them.

If Bhutan were a feudal society, its chances of quickly shaking off rigid forms and welcoming new ways would be slim. But Bhutan is not entirely feudalistic, although the relics of feudalism are there, in ritual and pageantry, in some social relationships, in autocratic rule. However, there is no hereditary nobility; there are the beginnings of an administrative clan chosen for merit; there is the *Tsongdu,* still far from being an effective arm of the government, but finding confidence in self-expression before a trusted leader, the king. And, perhaps most important, there is the will to change, to open the hitherto "Forbidden Kingdom" to new economic and political forces and risk the consequences of a gamble that has already caught the imagination of the Bhutanese people, a gamble from which there can be no retreat. It will not be long before the old Bhutan, the "Land of Dragons," "a realm that has been visited by only a dozen Europeans," [9] will shrink into the remote corners

[9] Nebesky-Wojkowitz, R., *Where the Gods are Mountains,* Weidenfeld and Nicolson, London, 1956, p. 162. (Translated from the German by Michael Bullock.)

of its beautiful valleys, and its medieval mystery and pageantry will be on the way out.

GOVERNMENT AND WORLD RELATIONS

INTERNAL POLITICAL ORGANIZATION

King Wangchuk is assisted in the administration by a national advisory assembly (*Tsongdu*) which was created eight years ago. About 25 per cent of the 130 members of the *Tsongdu* are government officers appointed to the assembly by the King. Included in the membership are influential lamas and the abbot of the chief monastery at Pimakha, who is a member of the ruler's council of eight. The rest of the body consists of village headmen elected for five-year terms from all over the kingdom. Several villages make up a Tsongdu constituency, and village headmen from each constituency choose, by agreement among themselves or by election, their representative to the assembly. In turn, each village headman is chosen for a three-year term by an election in which each family has one vote. For a country that is almost illiterate and knows little about democracy, the elected assembly and the village headman represent the basic foundation for giving the people a voice in the government. Above the village headman is a network of local administrators such as the *nyerchen* (tax collector), *zimpen* (magistrate), and *dzongpen* (district officer).

Several basic political-administrative problems currently challenge the nation. Extreme centralization and a top-heavy bureaucracy deaden initiative and adversely affect public morale. Weaknesses in the social structure contribute to the abuse of political power. The peasantry is largely exploited by the ruling class, which is composed of lamas or wealthy landlords. Since the aristocracy does not bear its proportionate share, the expenses of the government fall mainly upon the mass of poor population. There is no sizeable middle class to lend stability and to provide political leadership. Ninety-five per cent of the people are illiterate, and as a result they are not an effective force in the political life of the nation. Some steps toward political reform have been taken recently, but these are inadequate to meet the needs of the country.

On the surface Bhutan gives every appearance of being politically stable, and in a sense there are no politics in Bhutan. As noted earlier, however, the existence of a large Nepali population constitutes a potential political problem. One rudimentary political organization, the Bhutanese National Congress, does exist to express political feelings of the minority group, but because of limits placed on political freedom in Bhutan it operates from Indian territory.

INTERNATIONAL POSITION

As a weak power area, Bhutan has been the scene of British (and since 1947, Indian) and Tibetan or Chinese rivalry. Its strategic location on the perimeter of the Communist empire places it in the arena of power politics. As noted earlier, parts of Bhutan's territory in the Great Himalayan region are claimed by Communist China, and in recent years the border zone has been an uneasy one.

British influence along the southern border was firmly established between 1841 and 1864 by the annexation of the Duars. Up to 1904 the political relations between Bhutan and British India were conducted through the medium of the government of Bengal. After 1904 these relations were transferred to the British Indian political officer of Sikkim, resident in Gangtok, who was, at the same time, entrusted with political relations with Tibet. This change of authority was of great importance because it brought relations with Sikkim, Bhutan, and Tibet directly under the British Indian Government in Delhi. Since that period, relations between Bhutan and British India have been most friendly.

After the withdrawal of the British from India in 1947, a new treaty between Bhutan and India, signed in 1949, replaced the earlier agreement with the British. According to the terms of this treaty, Bhutan agreed to be guided by India's advice in her external affairs, while India accepted the responsibility for Bhutan's strategic communications and defense. The phrase "agrees to be guided" (used in the 1949 treaty) might be paraphrased crudely to state that Bhutan has given India the right to form its foreign policy. Further, according to the treaty, "the government of India undertakes to exercise no interference in the internal administration of Bhutan."

In addition, India agreed to substantially increase the annual subsidy (500,000 Rupees, or $105,000) established by the British.

Some members of the Bhutanese government, eager for direct diplomatic relations with friendly western governments—notably the United States—and the economic assistance that they expect to flow from such relations, argue that nothing in the treaty limits the right of Bhutan to have direct diplomatic relations.[10] In 1959 India advised the government of Bhutan against opening direct relations with a government other than itself. This advice is binding, and it must stand until India changes it or until the treaty is revised.

All of Bhutan's foreign aid comes from India. In recent years Indian economic aid has totaled nearly $3.74 million annually. In 1961 Bhutan launched a $36 million five-year plan for economic development with Indian aid. Fearful of global power politics, India has discouraged direct economic aid pacts between Bhutan and other foreign countries which might draw the small kingdom into entangling relations with outside powers and adversely affect her progress toward economic and social stability. India, however, does not object to negotiations with foreign firms or organizations for development purposes. Bhutan is negotiating with a Swedish company for the establishment of a paper factory, and the government is inviting French Roman Catholic nuns to help develop the kingdom's medical services.

In 1961 the Bhutan government requested the government of India to channel to them some funds available from the United States under Public Law 480. The Bhutanese were informed that there is no need for special diversion of P.L. 480 funds and that all the assistance Bhutan needs can be provided by India. India evidently does not want the United States to come into the picture, however indirect the connection. Moreover, India feels that in its present stage of development, Bhutan cannot effectively absorb additional assistance. China has repeatedly offered aid to Bhutan, but Bhutan has so far shown no inclination to accept it.

In the grip of progress, with visions of factory chimneys and

[10] "Bhutan: Thoughts of Sovereignty," *Far Eastern Economic Review*, Vol. 31, February 16, 1961, pp. 295-297.

the hallucinatory sound of busy wheels throbbing in their ears, the rulers of Bhutan are likely to move too swiftly. Even with good will, energy, and intelligence, they will discover that it is slow work to advance a society as anachronistic as Bhutan's.

A chief political problem, especially for India, is created by the predominantly Mongolian population of Bhutan, who have been traditionally oriented toward Tibet. Although the physical aspects of Bhutan—the Duar jungles and coniferous forests of the Inner Himalaya—are not very different from adjacent parts of India, the cultural aspects are distinct. People are dominantly Tibetan in feature. From the castle-monastery (*dzong*) which rises high above the floor of the deep valley, the Tibetan lamas blow their trumpets and beat gongs, and the prayer flags flutter in the air. In the past decade the Chinese Communists have taken advantage of this affinity to attract Bhutan toward Tibet. At first the Communist wooing had some effect, but the recent (1959-1960) suppression of the Tibetan revolt by Chinese troops has caused Communist propaganda to backfire.

In diplomatic terms, and quite apart from considerations of vital strategy, India treats Bhutan and the other Himalayan kingdoms as a regional unit within the Indian defense perimeter. India-Bhutan relations traditionally emphasize the strengthening of peace and security through frequent consultations and cooperative action.

A major difficulty in Bhutan-India relationships is the extreme dependence of the Himalayan kingdom upon India for its economic development and prosperity. It is essentially a relationship between a small and entirely undeveloped country and a partly developed, large nation itself in need of massive economic aid. What Bhutan needs is a great capital investment to improve communications, step up agricultural production, and develop its natural resources.

In his talks with Indian officials in February, 1961, the Bhutanese maharaja made it clear that Bhutan will have no direct dealings with China, despite Peking's refusal to accept India's privileges in Bhutan's foreign relations.[11] During 1961-1962 India took several

[11] Moorthy, K. K., "Bhutan's Blank Cheque to Nehru," *Far Eastern Economic Review,* Vol. 31, March 10, 1961, p. 429.

effective measures to strengthen Bhutan's defense in matters relating to China's threat and the border dispute. A high-level meeting held in February, 1961, presided over by Prime Minister Nehru and attended by the maharaja of Bhutan and India's defense minister and service chiefs, chalked out a new program for the discharge of India's responsibility for the defense of Bhutan. The strength of the Indian defense forces stationed to answer rapidly a call from Bhutan has been substantially increased. An intensive study of the facilities for Indian Air Force operations over Bhutan is being made. While airstrips capable of handling transport planes do not exist in Bhutan, large tracts are accessible to helicopters; more modern helicopters bought by India from the Soviet Union are being made available to the India defense forces for operations in Bhutan. At an invitation from the Bhutanese government, senior Indian military officers visited Bhutan in 1961 and made an elaborate survey of defense requirements. Following their advice, the Bhutanese government has now started a large-scale recruitment of militia from the native population, ingrained with the tradition of voluntary service, for border patroling to provide a constant vigil against Communist agents trying to infiltrate from Tibet.

The maharaja of Bhutan has agreed with India that in the present situation, when Bhutan's major problems are its dispute with China and the need for rapid communications development, it was not propitious to think of links with international organizations or western countries. Despite this agreement, Bhutan became a full participant in the Colombo Plan with Indian sponsorship. The kingdom also issued its first postal stamps in 1962, and the International Postal Union agreed to handle Bhutanese mail.

III

The Kingdom of Sikkim

". . . comprises every phase of Himalayan sceneries in all their glorious combination, scale, and magnificence."

—JOSEPH HOOKER

T HE Himalayan kingdom of Sikkim, with its population of 167,000, is most significant in view of its geopolitical implications. Tibet, Nepal, India, and Bhutan all touch its borders. Here, the scenic beauty of mighty snow-capped peaks, such as the 28,162-foot Kanchenjunga on the Nepal-Sikkim border, mingles with the romanticism of an historic past. There are huge, pine-covered forests bordering terraces of rice. Sikkim's simple, sturdy, and struggling people have preserved a distinct cultural and historical identity. Its villages of quaint wooden buildings hug rugged Himalayan slopes. Lights of little hamlets glitter like a myriad of glowworms in the evening. Old Buddhist monasteries perch on rocky shelves beneath the eternal snows. A mule train picks its way over the sharp rocks that pave the old trade route to Lhasa, Tibet; for here, in Sikkim, is a past living in the present.

From Sikkim's easily traversed passes, which give access to the Tibetan Chumbi Valley, the comparatively low (15,200 feet) and gently graded approaches of the Nathu La (Nathu Pass) lead directly to the core region of Tibet around Lhasa. The country occupies a commanding position over the historic Kalimpong-Lhasa trade route, the subject of a continuous succession of international arguments and treaties. Because of its location astride this vital trade artery, both India and Tibet have frequently intervened in its internal affairs. The British Indian government particularly exerted pressure upon Sikkim for access to Central Asia. It is a tribute to

Sikkim—not only to the present kingdom, but to Sikkim as the political core of the larger former kingdom—that the Kalimpong-Lhasa route between India and China remained open under Sikkimese control.

Aside from the trade route with its strategic and historical significance, Sikkim's location favors a dynamic role in international relations between the two great powers of Asia, India and China. Historically, Sikkim has figured prominently as a trade link between the Indian subcontinent and the heartland of Asia. More recently, it has been playing an important role in securing the Indian subcontinent against Communist aggression.

The study of the political geography of Sikkim must necessarily delve into two major aspects of the kingdom. First, the evolution of the Sikkim national state may be dealt with principally as factors of the political area. Second, the politico-geographic problems of the state itself, as one of the critical regions of the world, can be analyzed as an example of geostrategic location.

HISTORIC EVOLUTION OF SIKKIM

Sikkim, although settled as early as the thirteenth century by the Lepchas migrants from the Assam hills, came into being as a political entity in 1641. In that year the Lama of Lhasa, with the aid of two other lamas, converted the people of Sikkim to the Buddhist faith and appointed Penchoo Namgyal to be the first king, or *gyalpo*. The newly created kingdom established political relations with the Tibetan government, which had hitherto regarded Sikkim as a dependent vassal state. The first king reigned for 12 years; and little is known of his successor. Chagdor Namgyal, the third king, came to the throne in 1700. The "All-Victorious Thunderbolt-Bearer," as his name translates, was a pious Buddhist. He augmented the annual autumn offering to Sikkim's mountain deities by the great masked dance of the lamas, which is still performed. During the reign of the fourth king of Sikkim, Chogyel Gyurme (1717-1734), the "All-Victorious Inimitable King of Religion," hordes of warlike Bhutanese surged into Sikkim from the east, plundering the settlement and carrying off their inhabitants as slaves to Bhutan, the "land of dragons." After his death, Gyurme was succeeded by his minor son. During his minority, Sikkim was governed by a regent from Tibet. The regent reorganized the kingdom's administration, levied annual taxes, and drafted a code of law establishing the rights and duties of the citizens of Sikkim.

In 1780 Tensing Namgyal (the "All-Victorious Preserver of Religious Doctrine"), the sixth king of Sikkim, succeeded to the throne. His reign was ill-starred; the territorial integrity of Sikkim was threatened by the frequent attacks of the Bhutanese and Gurkhas on the Kingdom's eastern and western frontiers, respectively. The war-like Gurkhas had conquered Nepal in 1769 and were now seeking to extend their dominion to the east in Sikkim. The attacks from the east and west forced Sikkim to fight a desperate two-front war against the invaders. In those early years Sikkim was much larger in area. It included the eastern section (Ilam district), of Nepal, the Chumbi Valley of present-day Tibet, and the Ha Valley of Bhutan. Its southern frontier reached the plains of India and included Kalimpong and Darjeeling districts. But strategically placed as it has always been and sandwiched between warring nations, Sikkim lost much of its territory to invading Bhutanese and Nepalese in 1788 and 1789.

Tensing Namgyal's successor was Tsugphu Namgyal, who began his reign in 1793. During the reign of this seventh king, Sikkim came into contact with the British. In 1814 a powerful British force came to the aid of Sikkim; the Gurkhas were defeated, and the subsequent peace treaty (1817) established the Nepal-Sikkim boundary.

In 1835 the king of Sikkim "presented" the hills of Darjeeling "out of friendship" for the Governor-General of India, Lord William Bentinck, to the East India Company. Thus, all the land south of the Great Rangit River was ceded unconditionally to India; but the British government granted the king an allowance of 3000 rupees per annum as compensation, and this was raised in 1846 to 6000 rupees. Tibet, which had so far considered Sikkim as its vassal state, regarded the cession of Darjeeling to the British as an illegal action on the part of the king of Sikkim. Tension resulted between

Sikkim and Tibet, and Tibet prohibited Sikkimese monarchs from visiting holy Lhasa more than once in eight years.

In 1849 the maltreatment of high-ranking British officials traveling in Sikkim caused a serious crisis in British-Sikkim relations. Sir Joseph Hooker, a distinguished botanist, was imprisoned while exploring the Lachen region of Sikkim. Finally, British troops advanced to Tumlung, then the capital of Sikkim, and the British government gradually assumed control over much of the Kingdom. On matters of foreign policy, it exercised complete authority.

Despite territorial losses to Nepal, Bhutan, and British India, Sikkim survived as a distinct political entity. By the Treaty of 1861, Sikkim's political integrity as British India's protectorate was confirmed by the British. In 1886 the Tibetans penetrated temporarily into Sikkim. This action prompted the British punitive expedition to Lhasa in 1888, and on the conclusion of the expedition the British Indian government appointed a resident political officer to administer the affairs of the kingdom in conjunction with the local officials. Through its political officer in Gangtok, the British Indian government gained almost complete control of this Himalayan kingdom by reducing the power of the maharajah.

As a protest against the high-handedness of the British Resident, the ninth king of Sikkim fled to Tibet in 1892. The quarrel between the king and the Resident political officer was eventually settled, and the four Sikkimese monarchs who have reigned since then have been nominally the masters of their realm. The real power has been retained by the political officers, who have their residence at Gangtok, next door to the royal palace. This political-administrative measure has safeguarded Sikkim from further aggression by its covetous neighbors to the north, east, and west.

Since the little Himalayan Kingdom, forming a bridge between India and Tibet, was of considerable commercial and military importance to the British, visitors from Europe and America were allowed into Sikkim only by special permission. Permits from the Indian authorities are still required to visit the kingdom, and in many ways it has now become even more difficult for Americans or Europeans to enter Sikkim.

In 1947, after independence, India inherited the responsibilities of the British in Sikkim, and in 1950 India entered into a new treaty with the present maharaja, Sir Tashi Namgyal. The new treaty makes India responsible for Sikkim's external affairs (whether political, economic, or financial), defense, and strategic communication. Furthermore, just as in the British period, India, by treaty, has a representative permanently resident in Gangtok, the capital. The current Indian representative is a senior diplomat.

Sikkim faces two major politico-geographic problems. One is the demand of her own people for economic progress and representative government. The other is the pressure of Chinese Communism. In the following sections these problems are analyzed from the viewpoint of political geography, taking into consideration the chief physical and cultural attributes working to unite or divide ("centripetal and centrifugal forces")[1] Sikkim as a state.

THE PHYSICAL LANDSCAPE

The natural environment of Sikkim is generally inhospitable, though not sufficiently so as to preclude material advancement by an energetic people. Adverse surface features seriously impede human development over large areas; cultivated land amounts to only a small proportion of the total area of the kingdom. The climate is generally harsh, hampering economic development.

Sikkim is essentially an enclosed basin, nearly 40 miles wide, between two deeply dissected north-south transverse ridges, each of them about 80 miles long. To the west the remarkable Singalila ridge marks the boundary with Nepal and includes the peak of Kanchenjunga (28,168 feet). To the east the crest of the Donkhya range forms the boundary with Tibet. To the north the central basin is cut off from Tibet by the broad convex arc of the Great Himalayan peaks, built up of crystalline rocks, in which the Tista River rises. To the south it is blocked by the resistant rocks of the Darjeeling ridge, in India, through which the Tista has carved

[1] Hartshorne, Richard, "The Functional Approach in Political Geography," *Annals of the Association of American Geographers,* Vol. XL, No. 2, June, 1950, pp. 95-131.

a deep, narrow gorge running west of Kalimpong. This extensive bowl-like, mountain-girdled basin has been formed by erosive work of the Tista and its tributaries, such as the Rangit. Structurally, the Tista basin is "inverted," occupying the axis of an enormous over-folded anticline, the core of which is represented by the Kanchen-junga.[2]

The violent dissection of the Sikkim Himalaya occasioned by its location immediately opposite the alluvial gap between the hills of northeast peninsular India and the Shillong Plateau of Assam has been facilitated by excessive rainfall (over 200 inches annually) from the uninterrupted sweep of the moisture-laden southwest monsoon. The rivers (Tista and its tributaries) deeply dissect the central highlands of Sikkim, which are underlain by softer rocks. Thus, instead of a narrow gorge, a large basin has been cut back through the structurally weaker and less resistant crustal part of the central anticlinal axis of the Sikkim highlands.

Kanchenjunga range, a huge mountain mass some 12 miles south of the main chain of the Himalaya, constitutes a distinctive physical unit of Sikkim. It receives heavy discharges from the monsoon, and it is covered with snow and ice, often hundreds of feet thick. Pushed by the increasing weight of snow above and under the incessant pull of gravity, these masses of snow and ice move down-ward slowly in the form of glaciers or tumble over in great ava-lanches. These avalanches are an ever-present source of danger in northern Sikkim; and even in places of comparative security the almost continuous creaking and groaning of the moving ice and the roar of avalanches combine to create a sense of instability and apprehension. It is hardly surprising that the superstitious Sikkimese tribes regard Kanchenjunga as the seat of an all-powerful god.

An outstanding feature of the physical landscape in Sikkim Himalaya is the immense luxuriance and variety of vegetation. Along valley bottoms less than a thousand feet above sea-level, tropical growths flourish. From these valleys one may pass to the subtropical zone and higher up through the temperate zone to

[2] Pascoe, Edwin H., *A Manual of the Geology of India and Burma,* Delhi, Manager of Publications, 1950, p. 318.

an alpine region running up to the eternal snow. The wooded slopes of the outer ranges are studded with splendid specimens of different varieties of the great rhododendron, which in spring paints the forest crimson and yellow, and towering magnolia resplendent with starlike blossoms of waxy white. The forest-clad spurs and ranges of Sikkim, upon which the priesthood of the kingdom has built picturesque monasteries and shrines of Tibetan Buddhism, possess a singular attraction. Bright sunlight filters through a fretwork of rich green foliage, lighting up splashes of color where flowers grow on the slopes of moss-covered banks. Many-hued butterflies flash like living jewels from flower to flower, doing a mad dance of ephemeral existence under the stimulus of the sun-laden air. Every variety of foliage is seen, from the delicate feathering leaf of the acadia to the broad polished leaf of the up-standing *sal* (*Shorea robusta*). A host of parasitic growths cling to all the larger trees, ferns, orchids, and moss.

Contained within the Tista basin, and isolated from India by forest-clad mountains and from Tibet by the Great Himalayan range, Sikkim has retained a distinct identity.

CULTURAL ASPECTS

The presence of culturally diverse groups within Sikkim hinders the kingdom's cohesiveness. For instance, the lack of a common racial background is responsible for the disunity of the Sikkimese people. The term Sikkimese indicates a resident of Sikkim and has no linguistic or ethnological implications. Citizens of modern Sikkim trace their ancestry to a variety of Asian people—Lepchas, Indians, and Nepali—belonging to both the Mongolian and Caucasian racial groups. The native Lepchas, including the Bhutia and Tibetan-Dukpa, who overran Sikkim in the sixteenth and seventeenth centuries from Tibet, comprise only 21 per cent of the kingdom's population. The largest group is the Nepali settlers. About 1890 the British began to encourage immigration from neighboring Nepal. Today about 60 per cent of the 167,000 Sikkimese are Nepali Hindus. Disturbed by this influx, the palace (i.e., the

King) has now prohibited Nepalese from settling in the lush valleys of the north. Until recently the Nepalese settler did not have the status of a citizen, but the Sikkim Subjects' Regulation legislation of 1961 gave citizenship to these inhabitants of Nepalese descent.

The regulation, which came into force in the middle of 1961, was the subject of heated discussion in the State Council and provoked considerable agitation. The regulation approved by the Indian government was promulgated by the maharaja without the consent of the State Council. It divides the Sikkimese people into three distinct races—Lepcha, Bhutia, and Tsong. The new term "Tsong" is for people other than Lepchas and Bhutias. Since the term "Nepali" denotes citizens of Nepal, a new term for Sikkimese Nepalis was necessary to distinguish them. Sikkim's national party, dominated by Bhutias and Lepchas, demanded that the new term be reserved for people of Tibetan and Bhutanese origin and that the Nepali be called Sikkimese Nepali. The State Congress and the National Congress, dominated by the Nepalese, favored replacing "Nepali" with "Tsong." A section of this legislation empowers the government to deprive any Sikkim subject of his citizenship if he has shown by act and speech to be guilty of dissatisfaction or disloyalty toward the King. The above provision has been the subject of much criticism; opposition parties fear that it may be used to revoke the citizenship of opposition party leaders.

An urgent problem is to build closer relations between the Lepchas, Bhutias, and Nepalese, and the relatively small, but politically and economically significant, group made up of Indian traders and administrators. Lepchas have lost much of their land by the infiltration of Bhutias and, above all, by the rapid spread of Nepali settlers. In the old days they derived their livelihood mainly from the bounty of the forest. The forest provided plenty of game, edible fruits and tubers, medicinal herbs, and fibers that could be woven into fabrics. The Lepchas cultivated only small patches of the forest, cutting down the trees, burning the undergrowth, and planting the clearing with corn, buckwheat, and millet. The Nepali settlers, on the other hand, cut down wide areas of the forest for their paddy-fields. In consequence, the Lepchas' living space was continually reduced; the tribe became more sedentary, enlarging its fields and livestock. Hunting and gathering supplies in the forest lost importance; the forest ceased to belong to them, and they have to pay dearly for the large amount of timber needed in the construction of their traditional houses. As a people, Lepchas are honest, peace-loving, and unselfishly helpful. But their timidity and shyness, their naivety and tendency to individualism, have proved poor weapons in the unequal struggle they have had to wage for four centuries against interlopers from the north and west.

Conflict between the Tibetan Bhutias and the Lepchas have led to considerable disturbances in Sikkim in the past. The Lepchas have been pushed into the forests and lower valleys below 4,000 feet by Bhutias who have settled at higher elevations.

Racial distinctions thus represent a "centrifugal force" working to divide the Sikkimese people. However, despite these dissimilar racial groups, the religious factors and a common feeling of national consciousness have resulted in a certain degree of historic and cultural unity.

Tibetan Buddhism, the state religion, is followed by about 28 per cent of the population. Gangtok, the capital, is a colorful outpost of Tibetan Buddhism and possesses a fine temple, which is well maintained by the traditional rulers. The majority of the population, nearly 60 per cent, is Hindu. But in Sikkim, as in neighboring Nepal, Hinduism and Buddhism exist not only as separate religions, but also in a synthesized form. There is hardly any conflict between these two religions in this Himalayan kingdom. The official language is English, though comparatively few speak it; Sikkimese and Gurkhali are the languages of the people. Existing language divisions do not affect the over-all political stability of Sikkim; they are counteracted by the "feeling of kinship or belonging together" which centuries of living together has generated among the Sikkimese people. In contrast to Bhutan, where illiteracy is widespread, Sikkim has a rapidly developing educational program. The presence of a small, but politically alert, educated class adds to the feeling of national consciousness in Sikkim.

POPULATION AND SETTLEMENT PATTERN

The 1961 census revealed the population of Sikkim as 167,000, marking an increase of 29,000 since 1951. The average density of 59 persons per square mile is nearly the same as for the United States, but considerably less than for neighboring Nepal (174) and more than the sparsely populated Bhutan (47).

Sikkim's northern zone, an administrative area north of Chakung, contains only 65 towns and 7 villages with a population of over 500. It is the most sparsely populated part of the kingdom. Within the southern region, the eastern zone (east of the Tista River) with 126 towns and 37 villages of over 500 persons, is relatively thinly peopled as compared to the densely populated western zone (west of the Tista River), which has 254 towns and 65 villages.

The uneven distribution of population among the countless small valleys without adequate communication with each other hinders cohesiveness among the Sikkimese. The productive land is limited to clearings in the narrow, rugged mountain valleys, and the settlement pattern consists of dispersed hamlets on the lower slope above the cultivated land. Agglomerated settlements in the form of small rural villages with about 15 or 20 houses are found, isolated from one another, in the Great Himalaya and the upper section of the Inner Himalayan region. Here the scarcity of land level enough for building and cultivation, and the need for protection against the danger of avalanches and landslides, encourage the clustering of dwellings, often around a monastery which serves as the nucleus of the Himalayan village. In these isolated villages the physical environment limits the effectiveness of governmental control.

In addition to differences in settlement patterns, the High Himalayan and Lower Himalayan valleys reflect some contrasts in the living habits and standards of the people. The heavier concentrations of population in the Lower Himalayan region, especially bordering India, have been moderately susceptible to modern ideas and techniques and have had the broader view of the world. On the other hand, the population of the isolated High Himalayan

Kingdom of SIKKIM

Tibetan

Bhutanese

Lepcha

Nepalese

People of Sikkim

A Sikkimese Dancing Girl

Fortune-Teller in Gangtok

Rogers

region in the interior, with its large proportion of semi-nomadic people, has tended to remain self-contained.

Nearly 50,000 people, about one-third of the total population, are concentrated near the kingdom's principal urban center and capital, Gangtok. Ease of access permits Gangtok to be important commercially as well as administratively; it is the nodal point of the kingdom's political and economic core.

During the last decade the city, which contained a collection of wooden stalls and a few shops, has expanded greatly. Today fine stone houses, hotels, modern shops, and liquor stores, most of them owned by Indian merchants, line the main thoroughfare of the city. A new modern-style market (Lall Bazaar) has recently been completed. The urban landscape of Gangtok is marked by the royal palace, rebuilt a few decades ago; the villa-like residency of the political officer; the royal monastery, near the royal palace; and the newly-built Institute of Tibetology, which contains a valuable library of Tibetan manuscripts. The residency looks out on the nearby chain of the Himalaya. Below is the garden. Here, among gnarled trees and tall tree-forms, stand brightly painted Buddhist reliquaries and prayer flags swaying in the wind. The royal palace and the nearby buildings which house the offices of the Sikkim government offer curious contrast. On their outer walls, Tibetan characters interlaced to form diagrams serve to keep away demons and insure good luck. In the offices, which are decorated with images of Buddhist saints, typewriters clatter and telephones ring, but prayer flags flutter on the roof, and eerie constructions of animal skulls hang on the pillars by the entrance. These are "demon-traps" made by Buddhist wizards to prevent evil spirits from forcing their way into the Sikkim government offices!

THE KINGDOM'S ECONOMY

A reasonable measure of economic growth is basic for the political viability of a state. During the long period of political stability inside stable boundaries, following the Treaty of 1861, Sikkim developed an economy finely adjusted to the country's potentialities and opportunities. Significant advancement in Sikkim's economy began in

1888 with the appointment of the British political officer to administer the affairs of the state. Prior to 1888 there were no revenue system, no public works, and no program of economic or social development. The maharaja collected in taxes "what he required as he wanted it from the people; those nearest the capital having to contribute the larger share, while those more remote had toll taken from them by the local officials in the name of the Raja, though little found its way to him."[3]

The British political officer laid a basis for taxation, and a revenue system was established. In order to bring more land under cultivation, Nepalese immigration was encouraged by giving land on favorable terms.

As the revenue increased and money was available, the building of roads was the first development undertaken under the guidance of the political officer. In a few years, at the beginning of the twentieth century, it was possible to ride on mule track from one end of Sikkim to the other. In 1906, for the first time, Gangtok was linked with India by wheeled traffic.

Although the British did much to open up the country in the beginning, not much was done during the last 40 years of their protectorate over the little kingdom. Between 1907 and 1947 there were virtually no advances in the Sikkimese economy. After the withdrawal of the British from the Indian subcontinent in 1947, Sikkim became an Indian protectorate. India, which is sorely underdeveloped herself, is now the principal provider of economic assistance. India contends that economic growth is vital as Sikkim struggles to resist the pressure of Chinese Communism. The last seven years (1954-1961) have been a period of rapid economic development spurred by Sikkim's seven-year development plan under India's guidance. Success of the first plan prompted the launching of a second development plan for economic progress in 1961. This $17,073,000 second five-year plan is being financed entirely by India.[4] Although the emphasis is on transportation, various projects in-

[3] J. Claude White, *Sikkim and Bhutan; 21 Years on the North-East Frontier, 1887-1908.* London, Edward Arnold, 1909, p. 26.

[4] Government of Sikkim, *Second Five-Year Plan, 1961-1966,* Gangtok, 1961, 26 pages.

cluded in the plan would provide employment opportunities and training facilities to local youths for manning the technical services of the Government. In the first year of Sikkim's Second Plan (April, 1961-March, 1962) the actual development expenditure was only 10 million Rupees; the allotment for 1962-1963 is 15 million.

BASIS FOR AN ECONOMY

Agriculture has traditionally been the mainstay of Sikkim's economy since earliest times. Farming has been influenced by the nature of the terrain and by the diversity of climatic conditions, which in turn is due to wide variations in elevation and precipitation. The average yield is generally low, and the country is deficient in food grains. In Sikkimese agriculture attention is divided among staple cereal crops, commercial specialty crops, and animals and animal products. Rice and corn lead in acreage, but cardamom, citrus fruits, apples, and pineapples enter trade channels and so are better known. Potatoes, a major cash crop, are raised at an altitude of between 5,000 and 6,000 feet primarily in the southern region of the state. Sheep, goats, cattle, yaks, and mules are abundant; animals rather than crops support the population in the high mountain valleys. Beside supplying local needs, the pastoral industries furnish wool, skins, and hides, and surplus commodities.

In order to assist in the development of agriculture, a department of agriculture was started in 1955. The department has introduced improved varieties of crops from India and arranged for a supply of quality seeds. The use of fertilizers to step up crop yields and plant protection measures to save the crops are being introduced. Recent government encouragement, including the introduction of scientific methods, especially in fruit growing, has in some areas doubled and even tripled agricultural production. Agricultural experiment centers have been established at Tadong and Lachung, a potato farm at Temi, two cardamom nurseries at Gangtok and Rongli, a nursery for subtropical fruits adjacent to Gangtok, and an apple orchard at Lachung. A temperate fruit nursery at Lagyap has been renovated. A fruit preservation factory has started functioning at Singtam.

An important feature of Sikkim's Second Plan is to develop agriculture by disseminating knowledge of improved agricultural methods through extension workers. The plan provides for the appointment of agricultural officers in each district who will demonstrate better agricultural practices to the individual farmers. Further, the plan is designed to build up a panel of trained personnel from among the Sikkimese, who will gradually attend to the various aspects of agricultural improvement in their country.

FOREST RESOURCES

About one-third of Sikkim's 2,828 square miles of mountainous territory is forested, and forests are considered one of the kingdom's greatest assets. Forests occupy nearly 310 square miles in the northern zone, while in the intensely cultivated eastern and western zones forests cover only 203 and 235 square miles respectively. In the lower ranges and valleys, apart from what is left of the dense original forests, are valuable plantations of sal, simal, and bamboo. Acres of giant coniferous trees reach to the snowline in northern Sikkim, often wading waist high in the lesser forests of flamboyant rhododendron. Because of the few roads in Sikkim, and because some of the finest forests lie in the northernmost regions of Lachen and Lachung, exploitation has been difficult. Attempts to float the timber on the Tista River down to the receiving base and saw mill at Rangpo have failed so far because of intermittent floods and unpredictable weather.

MINERALS, INDUSTRIES, AND POWER

Since 1960 Sikkim's mining corporation has been instrumental in sponsoring systematic mineral development. Copper, lead, and zinc are mined in appreciable quantities.

No systematic survey of the industrial potentialities of Sikkim has been made. In Sikkim forests there is raw material for manufacture of paper pulp, matches, furniture, packing boxes, and tea chests. The Second Five-Year Plan provides for an industrial survey of the kingdom to determine possibilities of setting up industries based on forest products. In 1957 a Cottage Industries Institute was established in Gangtok to encourage local handicraft such as carpet making, weaving, traditional religious paintings, embroidery, and *papier mâché* work. At present, large factory establishments are limited to a fruit preservatory plant at Singtam and a distillery near Rangpo.

Sikkim's development has been handicapped by inadequate power supplies. Until 1960 only Gangtok had a small hydroelectric power station, which was established 34 years ago. In 1961 the Rangni Hydel Project, generating 2,100 kilowatts of electricity, was completed.

Work is in progress on four small hydroelectric schemes at Mangan, Rongli, Naya Bazar, Namchi, and Geyzing. Sikkim has considerable water-power potential. If hydroelectric power can be generated on a large scale, it is possible to supply electricity to adjoining areas in India, thereby greatly augmenting the financial resources of the kingdom.

TRANSPORT

Greatest emphasis of Sikkim's seven-year development plan was upon communications and transport development. Nearly half of the plan's outlay between 1954 and 1961 was on the development of road transport. Considerable stress on transport development in Sikkim is understandable. Without improvements in the circulatory system, the inaccessibility of various areas hinders the building of a sound and effective political organization in the mountain kingdom. Besides, without good roads and bridges none of the development schemes could be executed. Medical aid and disease control would remain static; the farmer's markets would be limited; education, if it could blossom at all, would remain compartmented. Ever since he can remember, the Sikkimese cultivator has lost the greater part of his profits because of the high cost of transport by mules or human portage. Now mechanized transport is at his disposal, and it is possible to reach almost every center of Sikkim within two days, as against four or five days or even longer, before the seven-year development plan period.

Above gorges full of the thunder of rushing water, new Indian-built bridges replace the swaying cradles of bamboo and cane that have served as bridges in Sikkim since man can remember. Cars and trucks oust pack animals and carts on new roads, and aerial cableways compete with the colorful processions of mule caravans that descend on Gangtok to pile its bazaar high with wool and exotic merchandise. These new roads supplement strategic highways, such as the Nathu La-Gangtok Highway, built by India under the India-Sikkim treaty of 1950. Gangtok has excellent road connections with Bagdogra (Siliguri), the air terminal in India for travelers to Sikkim.

The twisting mountain highway that runs from Siliguri, an Indian railhead, to Gangtok, Sikkim's capital, pushes for nearly 70 miles into the Inner Himalaya. This highway is the lifeline of the kingdom, which has neither railroads nor air fields. Along this road comes much of the food and processed goods that Sikkim needs, the equipment that is helping her to develop, the Indian military power that is protecting her frontiers, and the occasional tourist with news and ideas from the West.

Because of the rugged climb to 5,500 feet, most of the passenger vehicles on the road are American-made jeeps or the slightly heavier British Land Rovers. The drivers are invariably young Nepalese. At Rangpo the road crosses the Tista River into Sikkim by means of a narrow suspension bridge, bedecked with Buddhist prayer flags. It crosses narrow ravines over new bridges. The steep countryside traversed by the highway is a patchwork quilt of lush green trees, terraced rice fields, and groves of juicy oranges.

A major strategic road, now being constructed jointly by Indian army engineers and India's Border Road Development Board, is the 150-mile-long North Sikkim Highway. This motorable highway, which was completed by India in 1962, links Gangtok with the northern border areas. Although construction work on the road started in the fall of 1958, progress was impeded by various factors. Apart from engineering problems, one of the principal difficulties was the food supply for the large labor force (about 6,000 during a peak period) employed in northern areas, particularly during the monsoon months. Nearly 3,000 Tibetan refugees were employed in road construction work in 1961. This large labor force reflects the minimum use of road-building machines in the Himalayan area. The new road will not only strengthen the defense of Sikkim, but will also open the remote northern areas to trade and commerce.

In December, 1961, construction began on an alternate highway from Rangpo on the Indo-Sikkim border to Gangtok through Pakyang. It will ensure uninterrupted heavy vehicular traffic between Gangtok and India throughout the year. The present highway between Rangpo and Gangtok through Singtam is closed for heavy traffic during the monsoon.

POLITICAL ASPECTS

Two political aspects of Sikkim merit particular attention: first, the internal political problem of self-government and her ties with India; secondly, the broader problem of the relationship between India, China, and Sikkim.

INTERNAL POLITICAL PROBLEMS

In theory, the maharaja of Sikkim controls the state's internal affairs. The present 70-year-old maharaja is a frail, retiring Buddhist of Tibetan ancestry who prefers to pray, meditate, and paint. He has delegated most of his power to his 39-year-old son, Prince Palden Thondup Namgyal, heir-apparent to the throne.

The Sikkimese prince, educated at Darjeeling and Simla in India, recently married a 22-year-old American girl, Miss Hope Cook of New York City, a graduate of Sarah Lawrence College. The engagement was preceded by six months of negotiations between the governments of Sikkim and India because of the religious and political implications. In November, 1961, the state elders met in Gangtok to give their formal approval to the match, which was the first marriage between a member of the Sikkim royal family and a foreigner other than a Tibetan.

The Kumar—as the prince is popularly called—is aided in the administration by an Indian dewan, or prime minister, nominated by India. The dewan has now become an essential part of the kingdom's administrative machinery. There are also an Indian financial advisor, an Indian chief engineer, and an Indian director of the state distillery (an important source of revenue) and Indians at the head of other departments.

In recent years there has been some resentment in Sikkim against Indian domination, but more against the lack of a representative government. An elected State Council serves as an advisory body, but the major political parties want popular rule.

The Sikkim State Congress, at one time the kingdom's largest political party, was formed in 1947 and was originally affiliated to the Indian National Congress. Soon after the formulation of this party, the Sikkim National Party was formed with the patronage of the royal family. Both parties later split, and dissidents formed the Sikkim National Congress. The parent parties had once joined hands in cooperating with the administration, but the State Congress and the National Congress in 1961 expressed identical, somewhat radical, political aims and demanded a broad-based elected government.

Neither the maharaja nor the Indian political officer opposes self-government. Both contend, however, that Sikkim is not ready for self-rule. The Sikkim National Congress, the chief political party of the kingdom, has threatened to launch civil disturbances soon in an effort to force the maharaja to grant a constitution and representative government. So far, the chief obstacle to self-rule has been the division between the Lepchas, Bhutias, and Nepalese. In formulating any policy regarding popular representation, adequate safeguards have to be given to Lepchas and Bhutias, who form the minority. On the other hand, the Nepalese, who are in the majority in Sikkim, demand sufficient representation.

Sikkim's State Council, the state's advisory body, initially consisted of 17 members, 12 of whom were elected. In 1952-1953 general elections based on adult franchise were held for the first time in Sikkim's history for the 12 elected seats of the 17-member Council on a communal representative basis.

In 1958 a second general election was held. At this time the maharaja announced his desire that the government be "carried on equally by the two major groups of Bhutias—Lepchas and Nepalis

—without one community imposing itself or encroaching on the other . . . so that, with a constitution based on equality and justice, the communities should live in harmony with each other for the good of all his people." [5] Accordingly, the council was enlarged to 20 members, with six seats reserved for Bhutias and Lepchas, six for Nepalese, six for the maharaja's nominees, and one for the lama; the final seat was a general one. Of the 14 elected seats, Sikkim's National Congress won 4 seats; 7 were won by Sikkim's National Party and 3 by the State Congress. These political parties are still immature. In general, the political leaders are motivated by personal ambition; they are often unconcerned with the national spirit and national endeavor. Most Sikkimese leaders feel that in order to succeed they must be either avidly pro-Indian or aggressively pro-Sikkimese. The result is the general absence of the state idea among the leaders, and people often claim themselves to be Bhutias or Lepchas or Nepalese, but seldom Sikkimese.

Lately, through the ebb and flow of political maneuvering, the government of Sikkim has had one firm consideration—the preservation of Sikkim from internal political strife. Bhutias and Lepchas may be in the minority, but they are the original people, and their character is largely that of Sikkim. Accordingly, the administration has endeavored to safeguard their rights. The administration's policy is that the Nepalese, who are in the majority, should live as partners of the indigenous population.

The role of the Indian dewan in Sikkim is as difficult as it is important. As prime minister and chief advisor to the maharaja, his interest must be Sikkim's. Yet he is suspect—an Indian in Sikkimese clothing—so that useful and sympathetic as he may be, Sikkim's political parties would do without him.

SIKKIM, INDIA, AND CHINA

Politically, this Himalayan kingdom gives a picture of a country completely dominated by India, a picture often interpreted as the

[5] Speech as reported in "Sikkim: A Statesman Supplement," issued with *The Statesman,* Calcutta, June 2, 1960.

eclipse of Sikkim as a semi-independent kingdom. This interpretation is only partly correct. Geographically and ethnically, Sikkim has a distinct personality. Her traditions, customs, and beliefs give a character different from that of India. However, this distinct character can be safeguarded and preserved only by a powerful, but friendly, neighbor like India. This concept is particularly important in view of Communist China's attempts to destroy the centuries-old traditions and beliefs in neighboring Tibet.

As an Indian protectorate, Sikkim is on India's front line in the border dispute with China. Concentrations of Chinese troops have been reported along Sikkim's northern and eastern frontiers with Tibet. Yet Sikkim is the only area defended by India that is not directly involved in the border dispute. Sikkim's frontier was indisputably demarcated by treaties dating to 1890 between China and Britain, which then controlled the state. The boundary between Sikkim and Tibet follows the crest of the Great Himalayan range separating the waters flowing into the Sikkim Tista and its affluents from the waters flowing into the Tibetan Mochu and northward into the other rivers of Tibet.

China, which has laid claim to more than 40,000 square miles of Indian territory in the Himalayas, has made no claims against Sikkim. Militarily, however, the state is vulnerable and could be a gateway to the Indian plains if Chinese Communist aggression were to spread. Aware of this danger, in recent years India has rushed troops and arms into Sikkim. India is speeding the construction of roads, particularly into the northern valleys that formerly were accessible from the south only by mule track.

In response to Sikkimese demands for more responsibility for defense, India agreed in the summer of 1961 to allow the Himalayan protectorate to have a share in the defense of the border with Tibet by allowing the creation of a separate militia of about 280 native Sikkimese to be commanded, trained, and equipped by the Indian army. Likewise, India has entrusted the maintenance of some border roads to Sikkim. So far the defense of Sikkim and maintenance of border roads have been the exclusive responsibility of the Indian army. The protectorate's own militia of 60 men was designed primarily to guard the maharajah's palace. From India's viewpoint this delegation of responsibility has yielded significant psychological value, since, for the first time, Sikkim feels it has a share, however small, in its own protection.

Chinese Communist propagandists, meanwhile, have been offering "liberation" from Indian domination. They have aimed at the northern Sikkimese who have ethnic, and until recently, business ties with Tibet. To a great extent this campaign has backfired because of the Chinese suppression of the Tibetan revolt in March, 1959. Since then about 7,000 dejected Tibetan refugees have entered northern Sikkim. They are in close contact with those people the Communists are aiming at. The Tibetan refugees have been employed in road construction work in northern Sikkim. However, the presence of such a large refugee population has created several political and economic problems. Among other things, many Chinese agents have managed to enter Sikkim along with the refugees. Some of these agents have been detected and expelled. In 1961, several hundred refugees were settled in western Sikkim, and India has acted to alleviate Sikkim's uneasiness about its large refugee population by finding homes for several hundred Tibetans outside the protectorate in India.

IV

The Kingdom of Nepal

"Where India faces China."
—HAMILTON FISH ARMSTRONG

N EPAL, the largest of the Himalayan kingdoms, is but a small country of approximately 54,000 square miles—roughly the size of the state of Florida. It extends some 500 miles from east to west in an elongated rectangle along the arc of the Himalaya. The northeastern section of the country lies in the same latitude as northern Florida; the southeastern extremity, in the latitude of Fort Lauderdale; and Katmandu, the capital, in the latitude of Tampa.

Nepal is a land of great diversity. There are dense swampy jungles, rich rice-clad valleys, bleak alpine highlands, and towering snowpeaks within a comparatively few miles of each other. The northern interior has bitterly cold winters, whereas the southern Terai, less than 100 miles away, has a humid, subtropical climate the year around. Into this diverse physical setting, many ethnic groups have immigrated over the years to give the nation a racial and cultural pattern as varied as the land itself. One of the most pressing problems of the country is to create unity out of this diversity—to bring a national consciousness and stability of government into an area where every factor mitigates against such unification.

Like its neighboring kingdoms, Nepal has borders with both India and Tibet. They are long borders, and by nature difficult to cross. To the north the Great Himalaya presents a physical barrier which may be penetrated in only a few places. To the south the inhospitable swamps of the Terai and the rocky inclines of the Siwalik range impede passage into the interior. With the Tibetan plateau occupied by troops of the aggressive Chinese Communist government, the less penetrable northern border becomes geopolitically the more important of the two, not only to Nepal, but to India as well. The factor that contributes most to the strategic importance of this Himalayan kingdom lies in the fact that a strong Nepal can deny Communist China access to the rich Gangetic plain and can contain the Communist sphere in Asia north of the Himalaya.

GEOGRAPHICAL STRUCTURE

Nepal may be divided into three geographical regions—the Great Himalaya, the Inner Himalaya, and the Terai—which differ from the other kingdoms in detail only.

THE GREAT HIMALAYA

The height of the Himalayan range, the transverse nature of its valleys, and its bitterly cold winters not only contribute to the isolation of the country from the outside world, but also complicate communication between inhabitants of the region. As will be noted later, this intraregional isolation is an obstacle to acculturation between the various tribal and ethnic groups, and thus is an important factor in the continued diversity of the nation's population.

The landscape of the Great Himalaya, at higher elevations, is characterized by lofty serrated ridges, *cirque*-indented slopes, and sharp peaks produced by glacial action. At lower altitudes one encounters the deep river gorges, some of which, like those of the Kosi and Gandak Rivers, are several thousand feet below the crest of the adjacent ranges. Even the zone of the highest snow-capped ranges is deeply entrenched by rivers.

The deep, precipitous gorges of Nepal Himalaya, cutting across the highest elevation of the mountains, indicate that most of the Himalayan valleys antedate the mountain structure across which they cut. The fact that rivers such as the Kosi, Gandak, Kali, and Karnali drain not only the southern slopes, but also to a large extent, the Tibetan slopes of the Himalaya, is explained by their antecedent character.[1] The watersheds of the Nepalese rivers lie, not along the line of highest peaks in the Himalaya, but far to the north on the Tibetan plateau.

Climatically, the Great Himalaya is generally a region of extreme cold in which temperature varies directly with changes in altitude. But it protects the lower southern part of Nepal from the bitterly cold winds associated with air masses generated in the Central Asian source region.

In general, two climatic zones may be distinguished in the Great Himalaya: one from 12,000 to 14,000 feet; the other above 14,000 feet. From the standpoint of human occupance, only the first zone is important. Within the lower zone there is considerable variation in local temperature due to differences in solar insulation. Above 14,000 feet lies the zone of prolonged frost, where the limits of agriculture, even for hardy crops, is reached, and the tree line gives way to the alpine tundra.

THE INNER HIMALAYA

This region consists of an intricate system of ranges some fifty miles in depth lying between the Great Himalaya and the Churia Hills bordering the Terai. The Mahabharat Lekh, a singularly well-defined range of mountains extending from the Mahakali to beyond the Kosi Valley, may be taken as a prototype of ranges of the Inner Himalaya. Its ridges present a steep escarpment toward the south and a relatively gentle slope toward the north. The northern and northeastern slopes are clad in dense forest, succeeded higher up by a cap of snow. The southern slopes, except in the protected valleys, are bare, too steep to maintain a soil covering for the growth of forests or the accumulation of winter snow. To the north of the Mahabharat range, which encloses the valley of Katmandu, are the more lofty ranges of the Inner Himalaya, rising into peaks perpetually covered by snow.

[1] The term "Antecedent" is applied to a stream that has cut through land that has risen in its path, and so has maintained its course. In other words, it is antecedent to the present topography.

In the Inner Himalaya, climate undergoes a marked change with variation in elevation. The winters range from moderately cool to severe; summers are warm and rainy. The climate of Inner Himalayan valleys is well exemplified by that of Katmandu. Completely enclosed within the Inner Himalaya, Katmandu, located at an elevation of about 4,500 feet, receives an average precipitation of about 58 inches a year, most of which is brought in by the monsoon winds during June, July, August, and September. Temperatures range from an average 50° F in January to 78° F in July. The highest and lowest temperatures recorded in the last 26 years have been 99° F and 27° F, indicating no great extremes.

Rice, sugar cane, bananas, oranges, and other subtropical products reach their upper limits in the higher part of the Inner Himalayan valleys. The lower sections of the Inner Himalayan valleys are the areas of the most intensive farming in Nepal. The broad-leafed trees predominating in the moister, warmer sections of the Inner Himalaya tend to resemble those of the humid subtropical climate. In the higher margins these broad-leafed trees are replaced by coniferous evergreens.

THE TERAI AND THE FOOTHILLS

This third region, which has no exact counterpart in either Bhutan or Sikkim, consists of the Churia Hills, Bhabar, and the Terai along the southern border of Nepal. The Churia Hills, geologically a continuation of the Siwalik range of India, are covered with timber and savanna grass. These sparsely populated foothills rise gently from the plains to about 2,000 feet before becoming abrupt, almost perpendicular escarpments rising to an altitude of more than 4,000 feet. Within the zone there is a succession of narrow ridges, separated by more or less broad, longitudinal valleys whose strike is almost northwest-southeast. These valleys, known as "Duns," are a prominent feature of the foothills of Nepal. Southward lies the gravelly and fairly steep talus slope known as the Bhabar. In the latter zone great rivers swirl down from the Himalaya, and during periods of heavy rain millions of tons of silt and stone erode from the ragged contours of the higher mountains. Dense growths of trees flourish in the porous soil of the Bhabar.

South of the Bhabar and the Churia Hills is the Terai, a low, fertile, alluvial plain, a northward extension of the Gangetic Plain of India. It is 20 miles wide at its broadest point and extends over most of the southern boundary of Nepal. The northern part of the Terai adjoining Bhabar is a marshy region in which malaria is endemic; the southern portion, a belt some 10 miles wide, contains rich agricultural land.

The Terai has a fully tropical climate. In the eastern and midwestern Terai, rainfall averages more than 60 inches a year (falling mainly in the summer months), and a variety of crops such as rice, jute, sugarcane, mustard, tobacco, and corn are grown. The Terai is a densely populated area with more than 300 persons per square mile, nearly double the national average density of 174. The far-western Terai is a dry area; its average rainfall of 30 inches is subject to rapid evaporation. Here wheat and millet are the chief grains, and drought frequently causes crop failure.

Terai is a land of rivers. The Kosi, Bagmati, Gandak, and their tributaries are subject to frequent floods. The river alluvium, annually augmented during these flood periods, makes the soil of the lower Terai particularly fertile. However, the floods make communications continually difficult, farming precarious and uncertain. Furthermore, the high incidence of malaria in the swamps that they create reduces the efficiency of men and further limits the yield of the land.

EVOLUTION OF THE INDO-NEPAL BOUNDARY

For a long time the territory of modern Nepal was divided into a number of small principalities without a central government. In the seventeenth century the valley itself was divided into three principalities—one centered at Katmandu, another two miles distant at Patan, and a third six miles away at Bhatgaon. Prithwi Narayan, king of Gurkha, conquered the three principalities of the Katmandu Valley in 1769 and took unto himself the title of king of

Nepal. By the end of the eighteenth century he extended the Nepalese territory from Punjab to Sikkim.

During the second half of the eighteenth century, while the Gurkha rulers were consolidating the territorial area of Nepal through conquest in the Himalaya, the British were wresting political control of the Gangetic plains from the native Indian rulers. These two parallel forces—the British in the Ganges Valley and the Gurkhas in the Himalaya—confronted each other in the Terai.

The Gurkha king, Prithwi Narayan, was aware of the fact that the British East India Company, originally a commercial concern, had become a political power. Afraid that British traders might soon be followed by British soldiers and that trade would lead to political intrigue, Prithwi kept Nepal completely secluded from the British.

Warren Hastings, Governor-General of India from 1771 to 1785, tried to allay the suspicion of the Gurkha king in respect to the East India Company. However, after 1785, as the result of a series of border conflicts in Rautahat, Siuraj, and Butwal in the Terai, the relations between British India and Nepal became hostile. Nepal's traditional suspicion in dealing with the British, and her determined effort to extend Nepal's frontier toward the south, brought Nepal and the British into conflict. Earlier forebearance and moderation on the part of the British government were taken by the Nepalese as signs of weakness or, at least, of a reluctance to enter the rugged Himalayan area.

Convinced of the impregnability of the Nepalese territory and of the invincibility of Gurkha troops, the Nepalese government adopted a policy of systematic encroachment upon British territories. Attempts at an amicable settlement of the resultant border disputes in Terai were fruitless for want of straightforward discussions between the contenders.

During the early nineteenth century the British government abandoned the policy of moderation and forebearance which characterized relations with the Nepalese government in the last quarter of the eighteenth century. A war-like spirit was dominant in the court of Nepal, and the British government felt that the old policy was inadequate to meet the new situation.[2] It is, indeed, doubtful if continuance of that policy would have influenced the actions of the Nepalese government to any degree.

The decision to go to war over the boundary dispute was due mainly to Nepal's confidence in the fighting strength of the Gurkhas. Last-minute efforts to induce the Nepalese government to acquiesce to British demands for evacuation of the disputed Terai territory failed. The resultant Anglo-Nepali War of 1814-1815 terminated in the treaty of Sagauli, which was signed on December 2, 1815. The treaty was ratified in March, 1816, and gave highly important advantages to the British government.[3]

Under the terms of the treaty, the Himalayan districts of Nainital, Almora, Garhwal, and Dehra Dun were annexed by the British. In addition, Simla Himalaya was ceded to the British, and extensive tracts in the east were given to Sikkim. These losses reduced Nepal to approximately its present boundaries with Sikkim and India.[4] Further, the Nepalese were forced to accept a British resident officer at Katmandu. However, in 1858 a part of the Terai was restored to Nepal by the British as a reward for the help of Gurkha troops in the suppression of the Indian mutiny.

EVOLUTION OF THE NEPAL-TIBET BOUNDARY

In contrast to the well-defined boundary with India, Nepal's 500-mile border with Tibet is undemarcated. By tradition, the border follows the watershed range which generally lies north of the line of high peaks. However, Chinese maps have shown large parts of Nepal within Tibet, and Chinese governments—Imperial, Nationalist, and Communist alike—have seemingly considered parts of Nepal as Chinese territory.

Between 640 and 703 A.D. Nepal was regarded as a vassal state of the vast Tibetan empire, and as late as 1730 the small principalities

[2] *Parliamentary Papers,* House of Commons, Vol. XI, 1817, p. 8.

[3] Atchinson, C. U., *Treaties, Engagements, and Sunnuds,* Vol. II, Calcutta, 1863, pp. 110-112.

[4] Chaudhuri, K. C., *Anglo-Nepalese Relations,* Calcutta, 1960, p. 163.

of northern Nepal paid tribute to the Manchu emperors.[5] The Gurkha rulers, who conquered the Katmandu Valley in 1769, ceased to pay tribute and even invaded Tibet unsuccessfully. Under the treaty of 1792 they agreed to continue the payments to China. However, in 1854, the Gurkhas again attacked Tibet, this time successfully, and in the peace negotiations of 1856, Tibet agreed to pay an annual tribute to Nepal.[6] The Tibetan tribute was paid regularly until 1953.

In 1959 Communist China formally challenged the traditional Nepalese border with Tibet. Since then Chinese Communist troops have made several incursions into northern Nepal despite protests from Katmandu. In March, 1960, an agreement was signed in Peking under which the boundaries were classified into three sections: first, where the delineation of the boundary is identical on the maps of the two countries and the jurisdiction is undisputed; second, areas where delineation is identical, but jurisdiction is disputed; and third, areas in which there is disagreement on both delineation and jurisdiction. It was decided to appoint a Joint Boundary Commission to help solve the dispute. Nepal and China further agreed that armies of both countries were to be withdrawn $12\frac{1}{2}$ miles from the traditional border. However, in disregard of this border agreement, in June, 1960, Chinese troops entered Mustang, a Nepalese trading center about ten miles inside the border, overwhelmed the border patrol, killed one Nepali soldier, and captured 18 others. China apologized for this border clash, but explained that its forces were trying to liquidate Tibetan Khampa rebel elements which have been active along the Nepalese frontier.

As a result of protracted negotiations aimed at rationalizing the border, China and Nepal agreed, in October, 1960, to send a joint team to survey the border for boundary demarcation. The survey is essential because the territories involved in the China-Nepal border dispute are only vaguely known. Existent maps are inaccurate and, at best, show only rough boundary alignments. Neither country exercises effective administrative control over the

[5] Levi, S., *Le Nepal,* Paris, Ernest Leroux, 1905, pp. 239-261.
[6] Landon, P., *Nepal,* Vol. II, London, 1928, pp. 282-288.

disputed region. Fixing the boundary is, therefore, an extremely difficult task.

At the meeting of the Joint Boundary Commission in Katmandu in late 1960 it was suggested that the boundary should be drawn along known place names. But there were too few such generally recognized names for a 500-mile long border to prove effective. Nepal has pointed out some 150 place names, claiming them to be in Nepalese territory, of which China has claimed 20.[7] At the meeting of the commission in Peking in early 1961, a compromise is believed to have been reached on 100 names. Also, at this meeting the unanimous report of the joint survey team led to an agreement on territorial jurisdiction over grazing grounds near Rasua (in West No. 1 district) north of Katmandu. Nepal received her entire territorial claim here. However, the more important boundary problems in the Kimathanka area of the Dhankuta district in the east, and Nara Pass in the west, remained unsolved. In general, China was reported to be willing to settle the border disputes with Nepal, even to the extent of granting some concessions.[8] With the China-India border dispute in the headlines, the Chinese seem to feel that a settlement of the dispute with Nepal, as of that with Burma recently, would provide an excellent example of Communist China's desire for peaceful co-existence with her neighbors.

A boundary treaty could not be signed, however, without a decision on Mount Everest, the world's highest peak. In 1960 the Chinese laid claim not only to the peak, but also to an area south of the peak. The Nepalese were quick to voice their protest to such claims for Mount Everest, since it is one of their proudest possessions. When Premier Chou En-Lai visited Katmandu in April, 1961, he softened the Chinese claim and suggested that the peak remain a symbol of Chinese-Nepalese friendship. This suggestion obviously implied joint ownership, with mountaineering expeditions under the regulation of both China and Nepal. In consideration of Nepalese sentiment and of China's eagerness to resolve the border dispute, both countries have agreed, by the

[7] *The Statesman* (Calcutta), March 14, 1961.
[8] *New York Times,* May 14, 1961.

terms of the Sino-Nepalese boundary treaty of October, 1961, that Mount Everest shall remain on the border as currently shown on Nepalese and Indian maps. Nepalese politicians have accused the government of having abandoned Nepal's claim to the Mount Everest area in the boundary treaty with Communist China. However, the king has asserted that under the treaty, Mount Everest, "as before, is *still* Nepal's." [9] In general, the Sino-Nepalese boundary agreement affirms the principles of custom, tradition, known geographical features, and watersheds as the basis for the determination of the Nepal-Tibet boundary.[10] In June 1962 the Joint Sino-Nepal Boundary Commission began to erect boundary pillars on the ground according to the definite geographical points described in the boundary treaty of October, 1961.

POLITICAL EVOLUTION OF MODERN NEPAL

After the conclusion of the Anglo-Nepali War in 1815, the strong prime minister of Nepal, Bhim Sen, greatly increased the power of his office at the expense of the monarch. His strengthening of the prime minister's office paved the way for the establishment of the Rana line of hereditary prime ministers which ruled Nepal for more than a century. The first of these hereditary Rana prime ministers, Jang Bahadur, assumed office in 1845. Under his administration, relations with Britain became very friendly, and Gurkha troops were offered for service in the British Army. In 1850 Jang visited England and while there assured Queen Victoria of the friendship of Nepal for Britain.

From about 1850 to 1950 the hereditary prime ministers of the Rana family wielded supreme power under the aegis of titular kings. The Ranas were not progressive; they controlled great wealth, and the continuance of their position seemed to rest upon an economically depressed Nepal. Under these hereditary prime ministers the nobility flourished, but the masses were left to fend for themselves or to starve—often while struggling hardest to survive.

[9] *New York Times,* October 24 and 28, 1961.
[10] *Times of India* (Delhi), November 25, 1961.

As a result of a palace revolt[11] in 1950, the king regained his position of authority, and in February, 1951, King Tribhuvana's proclamation of a constitutional monarchy ended the reign of the 104-year-old Rana oligarchy. The period between 1951 and 1959 was marked by political instability and a rapid succession of governments, but it was also a period of persistent efforts by the king and some of the political leaders for the development of democratic institutions.

THE NEW CONSTITUTION AND ELECTIONS

In February, 1959, eight years after the proclamation of constitutional monarchy, a new constitution was announced by King Mahendra. Under the 1959 constitution, the king retained supreme executive power and extensive discretionary and emergency powers. However, the new constitution established a supreme court and two legislative houses. The Upper House was to consist of 36 members, one-third retiring every second year. Half of the members were to be elected by the Lower House and the other half appointed by the king. The Lower House was conceived to contain one member from each of the 109 constituencies (electoral districts), elected for a term of five years by the people. The constitution entitled all citizens over the age of 21 to vote, regardless of race, sex, creed, or caste. It provided for a cabinet, consisting of 11 ministers and 8 assistant ministers, to function as an advisory body, appointed by the prime minister and responsible to the Lower House of Parliament. Further, the constitution gave the king power to remove any prime minister who failed to retain the confidence of the Lower House, and empowered him to call or dismiss the Parliament at will.

In accordance with the provisions of the new constitution, the first general election was held in the spring of 1959.[12] An energetic program of education to prepare the people for voting was carried

[11] For a delightful narrative of the palace revolt, see Erika Leuchtag, *Erika and the King,* Coward McCann, New York, 1958.

[12] Joshi, A. B., "The First General Election in Nepal," *Parliamentary Affairs,* XII (1959), pp. 311-319.

to the most isolated mountain valleys. Though the people of the capital and other important towns had been increasingly aware of public issues since the palace revolt of 1950, political consciousness among the people of the interior remains undeveloped. To explain the significance of the election and the rights and duties of citizens, and to demonstrate electoral procedures, mock elections were held, pamphlets and posters distributed, and lectures and exhibitions organized at many places. The various political parties also contributed to the education of the voters and the development of public interest by organizing local units and conducting an active election campaign in all parts of the nation.

Because of the enormous difficulties of communication and transportation as well as the shortage of trained personnel to administer polling, the election was spread over a period of three months. The members of the Nepalese Election Commission had previously observed the conduct of election in India, an experience which proved of great practical value. Polling places were designed on the Indian model—one ballot box, marked with the party symbol, being assigned to each of the nine political parties that contested the election. To receive instruction radioed from Katmandu in outlying districts and to transmit returns to the capital, communication detachments of the British and Indian armies were placed at the disposal of the Nepal government. The polling stations were so distributed that no voter would have to walk more than two miles from his home to the polling booth. In sparsely-populated districts, this meant that one polling place had to be provided for every six or seven hundred electors. Each of the 109 constituencies (containing about 78,000 people) was determined with regard to existing administrative limits, communication facilities, population, and uniformity of culture.

The election was carried out without any disorder, and 43 per cent of the electorate (in some constituencies as many as 90 per cent) cast votes. The response of the electorate suggests that a recognition of their common interests and of the opportunities offered by the new constitution generated a new, though vague, spirit of nationalism among the Nepalese. This spirit could act to overcome some of the disruptive influences inherent in Nepal's physical and cultural geography.

Though political developments during 1959 were encouraging, Nepal's uncertain political stability continued to be threatened by the political immaturity of a nation with no past history of democracy, a nation plagued by economic distress and poverty and by a shortage of trained personnel for government. The conflicting interests among the people were reflected in the nine national political parties that contested the election. Political movements tended to oscillate between the extreme right and the extreme left. In the 1959 election there were few differences in the broad programs and promises of the parties that entered the contest. All parties promised land reform, development of unexploited resources, hydroelectric power, industry, improvement of health, education, and communication. In foreign affairs all parties professed a neutral policy of nonalignment with power blocs, friendly relations with other countries, and promotion of international peace. But significant differences emerged between the various political parties as far as their ideology, leadership, and public support were concerned.

The Nepali Congress, led by B. P. Koirala, laid great emphasis on socialist aims to be realized gradually through democratic means. It gave high priority to the redistribution of land and improvement of agriculture, village development, cottage industry, and improvements in health, education, and communication. It also favored protection of forest resources, promotion of heavy industry, security of foreign capital, and labor legislation. The United Democratic Party, led by former Prime Minister K. I. Singh, was more radical, proposing to liquidate landed aristocracy. Though frequently accused of alignment with the Communists, Singh has been critical of China and opposed the Communists in the election campaign. At the time of the election, the Communist party itself was weak, being confined to the Katmandu Valley and to the young labor movement in the Terai; since 1959 it has become considerably stronger. The right-wing Gurkha Parishad Party was supported in the election mostly by the Ranas and aristocrats. The oldest political party, the Praja Parishad, formed in 1936, was weakened just before the election by a conflict between its leaders, resulting in a split of the party.

A total of 964 candidates entered the contest for the 109 seats in the Lower House of the Parliament, 339 independents being qualified in addition to the candidates nominated by the various parties. Prior to the election it was predicted that no party would be able to secure a working majority, and that weak and unstable coalition governments would result. Despite these predictions, two-thirds (73) of the seats were won by the Nepali Congress, which contested all of the 109 seats in the election. The conservative Gurkha Parishad won only 19 seats; the radical United Democratic Party won five, and the Communists four. Every party president except B. P. Koirala of the Nepali Congress was defeated. In May, 1959, Nepal's first elected government, headed by B. P. Koirala, took office.

The new government had a sound political position and a sincere interest in coping with the nation's problems. It attempted to streamline the administration of the country, which had stepped into the twentieth century less than 10 years before. The Koirala government made efforts to reform land tenure by giving more security to tenants and compulsorily redistributing part of the larger, still semi-feudal estates. The new government's land program aroused the big landlords' opposition, and the growing popularity of the prime minister brought him into a clash of personality with the young king.

CURRENT POLITICAL DEVELOPMENT

On December 15, 1960, King Mahendra, dissatisfied with the growing popularity of the elected government at the expense of the monarch, staged a *coup d'etat* with the help of his "personal guards" and jailed Prime Minister Koirala and other members of the 19-month-old elected government. Further, he dissolved Parliament and suspended the fundamental rights guaranteed by the constitution. The king now rules his mountain kingdom directly with the help of a new council of ministers functioning under his chairmanship. Army officers faithful to the king are in charge of the key departments of the government, and the association of the army with the civil administration has been extended to the district level. The dissolution of the Parliament and the suspension of fundamental rights constitutes a sad set-back to Nepal's hopes of establishing a system of stable constitutional politics. The hope aroused in 1959, after the general election, that Nepal could at last look forward to a term of political stability under an elected government with a clear popular mandate, was lost with the suspension of the constitution.

Koirala's government had doubtless made the usual errors of inexperience. It was not immune from personal squabbling; and it had exposed its flank to criticism, from both left and right political elements, of its close links with India's leaders. But the only specific charge leveled against the elected government concerns its efforts to reform land tenure. The king's dismissal of the elected government may have been within his power, but it is doubtful if it was really in Nepal's long-term interests. It is clear that if reforms in the feudal system of land holding are halted now because of the immediate trouble it stirs up, the result will only be a more serious explosion later. In July, 1961, the king announced plans for a "guided" democracy from "below" by delegating authority to elected village councils. These should give the rural people some experience in self-government, although it is suspected that, in the absence of land reforms, village councils may come to be dominated by the big land lords. In October, 1962, elections to these village councils were completed.

THE POLITICAL
AND ADMINISTRATIVE ORGANIZATION

Although Nepal, in theory, is a highly unitary state, in which local authorities perform a limited range of functions under the control of the central government, in actual practice it is a loose union of almost autonomous districts over which the central government often fails to exercise full and effective political control. In many instances, these autonomous districts occupy distinct drainage basins, and their boundaries generally follow water divides. As late as 1924 no modern maps (or maps of any accuracy) for the entire country were available. The central area of each of the various districts was recognized, but its extent and boundaries were vague and undefined. During 1924-1927, Indian staff members of the Survey of India (European surveyors were not allowed inside the country) mapped the entire 54,345 square miles of Nepal from the Terai to Tibet, and excellent maps (at a scale of 1″:4 miles) showing the political divisions and physical features of the country were made available for the first time. The divisions shown in the Survey of India map sheets have been used by the government of Nepal. In recent years there have been a few minor changes, but the basic political-administrative boundaries shown on these sheets are regarded as correct. However, the Nepal government is considering the revision of the internal district boundaries in accord with distribution of population and with the principles of administrative efficiency.

At present, Nepal is organized into 38 political-administrative districts, some of which are further divided into sub-districts. These districts are divided into a total of 491 counties (*thums*).[13] In theory each of the 38 districts is administered by a governor (*Bara Hakim*) appointed by the king, but in practice the feudal governors in the outlying areas rule almost independently and owe only a nominal allegiance to the king. The large number of *thums* reflects primarily the localism of the individual settlements which is a strong and persistent feature of Nepalese life.

Realizing the need to associate the people with the administration, the central government announced plans for administrative reorganization based on the village councils (*panchayats*), which are elected for a two-year period. These elected village councils would form the base of the "democracy from below" envisaged by King Mahendra. The village councils will elect members to district councils, which in turn will choose members of the zonal council. The zonal council will send members to a national council. The national council, headed by the king, will have an advisory function

---

[13] See map in back pocket of Karan and Jenkins, *Nepal: A Cultural and Physical Geography,* University of Kentucky Press, Lexington, 1960.

and will take the place of Nepal's dissolved Parliament. The village and district councils will have wide administrative and development powers. The zonal council will discuss matters of national importance and send proposals to the national council for consideration. All the elections for this "council" form of democracy were due to be completed in 1961, but in early 1963 the National Guidance Ministry was still engaged in making arrangements for elections to the district, zonal, and national councils.

Meanwhile the king continues to rule directly with the plea that a strong administration is necessary for "a small country like ours to develop and advance in a world divided into two power blocs." But the king's despotic regime, which does not derive its authority from the people, can hardly provide a stable and strong administration.

Since November, 1961, widespread political unrest has prevailed all over the country. Guerrilla violence has spread rapidly in an attempt to force King Mahendra to restore a democratic government. More than 25 police posts were reported captured by the "people" opposing the king's rule between November, 1961, and January, 1962. Prominent Nepalese political leaders have accused King Mahendra of "insane and tyrannical oppression" in a "reign of terror and torture," and of making Nepal vulnerable to Communism by his domestic and foreign policies.[14]

Undoubtedly the disturbed political situation and lack of effective administration in remote areas have given to local Communists broad opportunities for infiltration and subversion. The chief danger lies in the fact that Nepali Communists could develop their own armed guerrilla bands and the kingdom may become torn between an anti-Communist, pro-India faction and pro-Communist, pro-China partisans.

• POPULATION FACTORS

As far as population factors are concerned, diversity rather than numbers is the chief politico-geographic problem of Nepal. Its 9½ million people (1962 estimate) are broken up into many identifiable

[14] *New York Times,* November 14, 1961; December 9, 26, 1961; January 8, 9, 13, 1962.

Kingdom of NEPAL

Sherpa Woman

Nepal has many structures which show a harmony of indigenous, Indian and Tibetan architecture

Gateway to Katmandu

Nepalese Dancers

Roger

ethnic groups living apart from each other in isolated mountain valleys. Each group follows its own cultural pattern, retaining tribal loyalties which make national unity difficult to foster. The enormous difficulties of communication—obvious in the lack of roads and modern transportation media—are complicated by local differences in language and an extremely high rate of illiteracy.

Population distribution in Nepal, as in several other nations of monsoon Asia, is extremely irregular. Few parts of the world are more empty than the snow-covered ranges of the Great Himalaya; few parts are more crowded than the Katmandu Valley. In the major areas of concentration the average densities range from 500 to 600 per square mile. Densely populated areas are concentrated in two broad regions: first, in an almost continuous zone along the southeastern Terai, and second, in a band of mountainous country stretching from the eastern border to west-central Nepal, in which populous valleys, sparsely peopled hill slopes, and empty ridge tops form a complex pattern of distribution. Katmandu Valley, the major political, economic, and cultural focus, has a density of over 2,000 persons per square mile. Within its 209 square miles live five per cent of the nation's population; and urban Katmandu has a population density of 47,783 persons per square mile. Outside of the Katmandu Valley there are fairly large concentrations in most of the river valleys of eastern and central Nepal.

The large-scale migrations of Mongoloid groups from Tibet and Indo-Aryan people from northern India, which apparently accompanied the early settlement of Nepal, has produced a complex racial pattern. The great variations in land form and the difficulty of communication between different regions have preserved distinctions of physical appearance among the population groups, roughly corresponding to the areas of Tibetan and Indian migration and the degree of intermixture between these peoples. Thus, darker coloring and taller stature is predominant in the south, whereas lighter coloring and short stature characterize the north. Racial origin is important in the hierarchy of social groups. Indo-Aryan ancestry has been a source of prestige in Nepal for centuries, and the ruling families have been of Indo-Aryan and Hindu background.

Although the political unification of the kingdom took place late in the eighteenth century, some of the tribal organizations have remained more or less intact. Some 10 or 12 major ethnic groups and a number of smaller ones are represented in the population. Many of the tribes have developed a strong caste system derived from the Hindu culture, and all Nepalese tribes have a sense of tribal identification which mitigates against the development of a Nepalese nationalism.

• Among the major tribal groups are Newars, Gurung, Magar, Rais, Limbus, Sunwars, Bhutias, and Tharus. The Newars, concentrated in and near the Katmandu Valley, are the principal native mercantile group in Nepal. They represent an important political force in the country. The Gurungs, a pastoral people closely resembling the Tibetans, are found mainly on the southern slopes of Annapurna, Himal Chuli, and Ganesh Himal. The Magars inhabit the areas directly south and west of the Gurungs in the Palpa district and adjoining areas west of the Katmandu Valley. The famous Gurkha soldiers of Nepal come mainly from the Gurung and Magar tribes. The Rais, Limbus, and Sunwars inhabit the eastern mountains. Bhutia includes a number of ethnic groups made up of recent Tibetan migrants. They live close to the Tibetan border in the upper reaches of the river valleys. The Sherpas are the best known subdivision of this group. The Tharus are a group of people, possibly Dravidian in origin, who are widespread in the Terai, where they have developed an immunity to the malaria of the region.

Religious differences, which are of great social, economic, and political significance in Nepal, introduce another element of complexity in the country's political geography and make national cohesiveness more difficult to achieve. The distribution of religious groups does not follow the lines of ethnic division; many of the tribes are divided as to religion.

The two major religions of Nepal are Buddhism and Hinduism, but no sharp line can be drawn between the two faiths in the lower Himalayan valleys, for in this region Buddhism and Hinduism have become more or less fused, the practices and beliefs as well as the gods and shrines of both being equally worshipped by the people.

Hinduism, the religion of the ruling class since the Gurkha conquest of 1769, claims more adherents in Nepal than any other faith. Within the area of Buddhism, two regions can be distinguished on the basis of ritual and belief. The northern region is in general the zone of lamaistic Buddhism, very similar to that practiced in Tibet. To the south, in the lower Himalayan valleys, Buddhism has been strongly influenced by Hinduism. Further religious disunity among the Buddhists is due to the existence of religious beliefs alien to Buddhism or Hinduism. Prominent among such beliefs unconnected with orthodox Buddhism is the cult of mountain gods which invests each mountain peak with a deity and which rules over the surrounding land.

The cultural diversity is complicated further by the large number of mutually unintelligible languages spoken in Nepal. The principal language of an ethnic group is further divided into numerous sub-languages and dialects. The multiplicity of languages creates serious barriers between peoples and plays a significant role in promoting regional and tribal sentiment. The lack of a national language makes the reduction of illiteracy far more difficult in Nepal than is the case in a country with one common language. It further retards any government effort to improve public health and economic welfare through educational programs.

There are notable regional distributions of major language groups. The languages of the Terai and the lower Himalayan valleys belong to the Indo-Aryan family. Within this family Pahari is dominant in the Lower Himalaya, while Hindi similar to that spoken in Bihar and Uttar Pradesh of India is prevalent in Terai.

In the Great Himalaya, the languages are Tibeto-Burman in origin. Of these, Newari is the most important. There is a considerable body of writing in Newari in spite of the determined effort of the Gurkha conquerors to suppress Newari literature. Other Tibeto-Burman languages include Magarkura, Gurungkura, and Kiranti. A number of Tibetan dialects spoken by the Bhutias along the northern frontier contribute further to linguistic disunity. The official language of the nation is Nepali, a language which has certain features in common with Hindi. It has borrowed words from the Tibeto-Burman languages and now presents a mixed character, but it is derived from Sanskrit and written in the Dev Nagari script. Spoken by many people as a second language, Nepali seems to be slowly replacing the tribal languages in areas near the Katmandu Valley.

ECONOMIC DEVELOPMENT

The economy of Nepal is basically agricultural, and it seems likely to remain so for a long time. The development of industry is limited by the availability and accessibility of natural resources and the low level of technological skills possessed by the people. The difficulty of establishing a transportation network across the deep gorges and transverse ridges of the Nepalese landscape is a serious limiting factor, even considering the inventory of the natural resources of the country. Despite these handicaps, modern Nepal faces the urgent problem of creating an economic system that will serve the wants of people who are fast becoming aware of the material goods of the outside world. Unless it achieves that goal, an already depressed economic situation will become worse, creating serious internal dissensions and further aggravating instability.

LAND USE AND AGRICULTURE

In Nepal, where intensive cultivation has been going on for many centuries, much of the potentially arable land—slightly over 10 per cent of the total area—is already under cultivation.[15] Notwithstanding this intensive farming, Nepal has far to go before its 9½ million people can be assured an adequate diet. Most of the cultivated land is located in the humid Terai plain, which contains nearly two-thirds of the arable land; in the southeastern Terai 70 to 80 per cent of the land is cultivated. In eastern Nepal areas now under cultivation include considerable land that, for ecological and topographical reasons, should be under pasture or forest. On the other hand, some areas in the west that are well suited for farming are

[15] Karan, Pradyumna P., "A Land Use Reconnaissance in Nepal by Aerofield Techniques and Photography," *Proceedings, American Philosophical Society,* Vol. 104, April, 1960, pp. 172-187.

uncultivated because of uncertainty of rainfall. There is a general lack of irrigation facilities, only one-fifth of the cultivated land being irrigated at present. Because of differences in physical conditions, a variety of crops are grown. An estimated 55 per cent of the harvested land is in rice, 20 per cent in corn and millet, and 10 per cent in wheat.[16] Smaller proportions of the arable land are devoted to the production of potatoes, oil seeds, tobacco, jute, sugar cane, buckwheat, and vegetables.

The hot and humid eastern portion of Terai is the outstanding agricultural area of Nepal. Here an extended monsoon entailing heavy rainfall permits cultivation of two or three crops per year. Two crops of rice are common, and jute and sugar cane are also raised. This area is economically the most valuable one in Nepal; most of the Nepalese exports of agriculture products originate in eastern Terai.

The fertile valleys of the Inner Himalaya, most of them at altitudes of 4,000 to 5,000 feet, have deep, rich soils and support intensive farming. The complex geographical pattern of these intensively cultivated and densely populated valleys has resulted in the development of several widely scattered core areas. Among these, the Katmandu and Pokhara valleys are of considerable importance in terms of centers of political power and influence within Nepal. In the sparsely populated higher valleys of the Great Himalaya, up to 14,000 feet, agriculture is based on the cultivation of potatoes and the raising of herds. These areas are relatively backward, with very little resource development. Until recently, they were economically oriented toward Tibet.

Increased food production to meet the needs of the growing population is essential to maintain economic and political stability in Nepal. So far the Nepalese government has not made impressive headway in its battle to overcome the obstacles toward increasing food production. Nearly 10 per cent of the total land area under cultivation represents a fairly high percentage in view of the moun-

---

[16] Bowers, G. V., *Agricultural Development in Nepal,* U. S. Department of Agriculture, Washington, D.C., 1953, pp. 24-28.

tainous nature of the country. Land-use surveys[17] indicate little possibility of additional food production by the expansion of cultivated land. In Nepal food production can be augmented by increasing the crop in areas already in cultivation. However, attempts to raise crop yields are hindered by the shortage of fertilizers, failure to rotate crops, and lack of irrigation facilities.

Progress in agriculture and food production is further limited by a complex and burdensome system of land tenure. Until quite recently, land taxes and rents were levied without regard to the size or productivity of the holdings. This system, coupled with the privileged status of certain lands, placed the tax burden on the small landholder and the tenant. The century-old *birta* lands (rent-free holdings) of members of the ruling Rana class were abolished during 1960-1961. Attempts are being made to revise the system of land taxes so as to foster agricultural progress.

A final factor hindering agricultural development is the widely prevalent rural indebtedness. In the years of low yield due to uncertain rainfall, tenant farmers are forced into debt in order to pay the rent. As the rate of interest is high, it is difficult for the average farmer to repay his loan. Working under a burden of debt, the Nepalese farmer can make little improvement on the land, and progressively poorer yields involve him in a vicious cycle which has its effect on the total productivity of Nepalese agriculture. A Royal Land Reforms Commission (under the chairmanship of former Premier Tanka Prasad Acharya) was appointed in 1961 to make recommendations to the government for agricultural improvement by the middle of 1962.

As a result of the country's strategic location, both the United States and India have made important contributions toward alleviating Nepal's food shortages. Under the Nepal-U.S.A. Irrigation Fund, one large multipurpose development has been completed in the Rapti Valley, and several small irrigation projects are under

[17] Karan, Pradyumna P., and William M. Jenkins, Jr., "Population, Land Utilization and Possible Expansion of Cultivated Area in Nepal," *Pacific Viewpoint,* Vol. 2, No. 1, March, 1961, pp. 41-58.

construction in the Terai for raising agricultural productivity. The Rapti Valley multipurpose development, modeled on the lines of the Tennessee Valley Authority, has enabled reclamation of considerable land for agriculture. India's multipurpose Kosi and Gandak projects will also irrigate large areas of Nepal. In addition, India is helping with several other projects designed to increase the overall agricultural efficiency and food production in Nepal. In 1962 the United Nations Food and Agricultural Organization in its effort to aid Nepal in agricultural planning began a census of agriculture covering major crops and livestock.

MINERALS AND POWER

Although surveys are incomplete as to the actual extent of natural resources of Nepal, it is obvious that it has few of the essentials for industrialization. Coal, iron, mica, copper, and cobalt have been found in various parts of the country, but proven reserves are small and often of poor quality. Economically speaking, most of the known deposits of these minerals seem unsuited for large-scale mining development. Most are small deposits of medium- or low-quality ores, and they are located in areas where access is difficult and transport costly for profitable commercial exploitation.[18] In addition, the highly faulted and folded geological structure of the country makes continuous deposits of minerals unlikely.

Several countries are helping Nepal in a geological survey program to discover mineral deposits. The Swiss government was the first to assist in surveying the mineral potential of the Kingdom. Later the United Nations provided an expert to conduct a general geological mapping. The United States, through its International Cooperation Administration, advised the Nepal government on mineral policies and trained local technicians in field work. With American aid, a Bureau of Mines, with a new, modern, fully-equipped laboratory, has been set up in Katmandu. The bureau has a competent staff of geologists and engineers, all graduates of Indian

[18] Pearson, G. E., "Nepal's Mining Prospects," *Far Eastern Economic Review,* Vol. 34, October 19, 1961, pp. 170-171.

universities, who have received additional training in American universities. Several long-term mapping projects have been undertaken by the Geological Survey of India.

Since large reserves of high-quality coal are lacking and mineral oil is unavailable, hydroelectric plants promise to be the basic source of Nepal's energy production. Undoubtedly, for its small area, Nepal has a comparatively high hydroelectric potential. The mountainous surface of the country and the moderately high precipitation favor the development of water power in almost every district. Because of the lack of statistics concerning river flow, no estimate of the amount of potential power is available. However, it should be kept in mind that much of the water power potentially available in Nepal cannot now be developed economically because it is too far from markets or calls for too great an expenditure in development.

Because of lack of capital and technological resources to harness water power and the absence of industry to use it if available, there has been little hydroelectric development. The total installed hydroelectric capacity is only 1,350 kilowatts, most of it concentrated in the Katmandu Valley. There are small plants producing both hydroelectric and thermal power in the vicinity of Biratnagar. Nepal has ambitious plans to develop water-power resources, but it is doubtful that these plans will mature in the near future because of lack of capital, equipment, and trained personnel. At present, most of the sites cannot be reached by motorable roads, and there is little demand for power outside Katmandu and Biratnagar.

In January, 1962, the United Nations Special Fund agreed to assist Nepal with a contribution of U.S. $914,000 for a three-year survey of hydroelectric power potential of the Karnali River basin in western Nepal. In addition to indicating the most suitable sites for the location of power stations, this survey will report possibilities of the export of surplus power to India. It is estimated that the income from the sale of power generated by the Karnali project would be greater than the present total revenue of Nepal.[19]

[19] Chandramohan, A. T., "Nepal: U.N. Aid to River Project," *Far Eastern Economic Review,* Vol. 35, February 8, 1962, p. 320.

MANUFACTURING

Most of the manufacturing carried on in Nepal is of the cottage industry type, employing relatively simple processes. Unlike true industrialized areas, Nepal has no complex division of labor, nor to any appreciable extent is value added by manufacturing processes. The total number of factories in the entire country is small, and they employ approximately 20,000 workers—an insignificant fraction of the Nepalese population. The amount of subscribed capital invested in industry is a mere four million dollars. In terms of capital investment, the largest industry is jute manufacture; cotton industries and food processing occupy second and third positions, respectively. These three industries represent three-fourths of the total investment.

Increased industrialization is regarded as a means of raising the standard of living in Nepal, and the official development plans have laid considerable emphasis on industrial development. As has been noted, however, the nation has relatively little in the way of mineral wealth upon which to base industrialization; it is not an agricultural surplus area; its people are not experienced with machines, and there is a general absence of skilled factory workers and trained personnel. The purchasing power of the population is little, and Nepal will find it very hard to break into already established markets in India. Transportation is poorly developed. Instability of the government and the general political situation deter both local and foreign investment. However, in August, 1961, the Nepal government and the Indian industrial house of Birlas reached an agreement on the construction of a modern textile mill estimated to cost nearly four million dollars.[20] This mill, expected to go into production within 18 months to two years, is the first large foreign investment designed to industrialize the country. The new mill will be the biggest industrial enterprise in Nepal, with an estimated capacity of 20 million yards of cloth annually woven on 400 looms and 15,000 spindles. Nepal is one of the countries with which the United States has an Investment Guarantee Agreement. The chances of American private investment coming into Nepal are remote, how-

[20] *Far Eastern Economic Review,* Vol. 33, August 10, 1961, p. 259.

ever, though it is likely that American firms based in India may extend their operations into Nepal. So far United States aid for specific industrial resource development programs has been over a million dollars. In addition, the U.S. government's Export-Import Bank has granted Nepal a loan of one million dollars in Indian Rupees to augment the Nepal Industrial Development Corporation's industrial financing capabilities by allowing it to purchase equipment in India.[21]

Nepal on its part has revised its factories law to foster industrialization. In 1961, for the first time in its history, Nepal introduced arbitration by tribunal in the case of industrial labor disputes. This method of settlement is provided for by the Factories and Factory Workers Amendment Act promulgated by King Mahendra in August, 1961. Although industrial employment is scarce in Nepal, the act seeks to provide some basis for industrial growth in the country. Only two significant industrial projects are now scheduled to be completed in the future. With the aid of Communist China, a cement factory and a paper plant are to be built. The sites for these plants have not been selected, and since the Nepalese government, faced with financial crisis, is unable to meet her share of costs (local costs such as land, labor, and approach roads to industrial sites), the establishment of the two industrial plants seems destined to considerable delay. In order to encourage industrial growth the government made provisions to exempt large and small industries from business profits tax to the extent of 25 per cent and 50 per cent, respectively. Furthermore, industrial estates are being set up at Patan in the suburbs of Katmandu under Indian aid and at Balaju, also in the suburb of Katmandu, by Nepal's Industrial Development Corporation. The government also plans to double the production of the American-built sawmill at Hetaura, Nepal's growing industrial township.

TRANSPORT AND TRADE PROBLEMS

Beside hindering the development of trade and industry, the lack of an interregional transport system is Nepal's great handicap in

[21] *Far Eastern Economic Review,* Vol. 33, September 21, 1961, p. 588.

welding the country into one nation. It would be difficult to conceive of a pattern of internal transport that would more seriously hinder the achievement of political unity and coherence than does that of Nepal. Most of the overland routes from Katmandu to outlying districts in the east and west go across the Indian border, through Indian territory, and back into Nepal. As a result of the slow and scanty circulation pattern, the regions beyond the Katmandu Valley and adjacent areas lie outside the effective national territory of Nepal from the point of view of political control. Thus, Katmandu exercises *de jure,* but not *de facto,* political control over the outlying parts of Nepal.

Nepal's only railroad is a narrow-gauge line 29 miles long from Raxaul at the Indian border to Amlekhganj near the foothills.

The government-owned and operated ropeway, an electrically powered aerial cableway, transports cargo in baskets from Amlekhganj railhead to Katmandu. The original capacity of this ropeway, built in 1924, was 8 tons per hour, but constant wear and tear on the moving parts has reduced capacity to 5.6 tons per hour. It operates 12 hours per day, delivering nearly 60 tons of goods daily to the Katmandu Valley. American aid is now being used to increase the capacity of this ropeway.

Until 1956 Katmandu was an isolated capital having no modern surface transport link with the rest of the world.[22] In that year the Tribhuvana Raj Path linking Katmandu with India was completed. A number of unpaved fair-weather roads serve the Terai, linking the local trade marts with railheads in India.

Air transport was introduced in Nepal in 1950 with the construction of a fair-weather landing strip at Gauchar, in Katmandu Valley, which enabled inauguration of daily Patna-Katmandu DC-3 service. The air service has gradually expanded in other parts of Nepal with construction of fair-weather airstrips in outlying areas of the country. The United States foreign aid program is helping in the development of Nepal's domestic air service. In recent years the United States has supplied airplanes to Nepal and has

[22] "Nepal Turns Back on Its Seclusion," *New York Times,* February 21, 1962.

installed navigational aids at the newly constructed air strips, including one at Mustang near the Tibetan border.

In most of the country, coolies or pack animals constitute the only available transport system. The high cost of coolie and pack-animal transport on the mule paths and narrow trails of the mountains severely restricts the flow of trade, peoples, and ideas so essential to the political organization of a national territory. A poor circulatory system remains one of the significant factors limiting a stronger political organization of Nepal's territory. Progress is impeded and local regionalism fostered by the inaccessibility and isolation of much of the country from the political core of Katmandu. To alleviate the situation would require considerable amounts of capital and material. It is unlikely that the transportation network will greatly improve in the immediate future. The Soviet Union has promised to construct an east-west highway running across Nepal, but as yet no actual work has been done on this project.

In the fall of 1961 Communist China and Nepal concluded an agreement for the construction of a highway linking Katmandu with Lhasa, the capital of Tibet. Under the agreement, China will grant Nepal the equivalent of $9,800,000 over the next five years. The first installment was received by Nepal on July 1, 1962, and the final installment will be paid on June 30, 1966. No compensations, conditions, or privileges are attached to the aid. The aid will be utilized to construct the section of the highway that falls within Nepalese territory. The assistance supplied by China will include: (1) experts and technicians; (2) the necessary machines and materials for construction; and (3) the training of Nepalese technicians and skilled workers both in Nepal and in China.

Considerable apprehension has been expressed in India and other countries because the agreement will admit an undisclosed number of Communist experts and technicians to Nepal. India, which has border disputes with China, views this highway project as a potential threat to her security. The "road of friendship" linking Katmandu and Lhasa is expected to be named Mahendra Raj Path. The memory of the late King Tribhuvana is honored by the Indian-built Tribhuvana Raj Path linking Katmandu with India.

King Mahendra sees no subversive threat from Communist China in the construction of the Lhasa-Katmandu highway. Many Nepalese express the view that they have been economically dependent upon India for too long. They insist that a land-locked Nepal should develop alternate outlets to the rest of the world.

TRADE

Except in the larger population centers, internal commerce in Nepal is largely on a barter basis. Nepal has little foreign trade with nations other than India because of three factors: an unstable currency which necessitates payment in Indian currency; the small size of Nepal's demand for goods manufactured outside India; and its dependence on Indian railways and ports for shipments from abroad.

Table 1   *Direction of Nepal's Foreign Trade*
(in percentages, excluding invisibles)

	Imports		*Exports*		*Total Trade*	
	1959-1960	*1958-1959*	*1959-1960*	*1958-1959*	*1959-1960*	*1958-1959*
India	93.88	97.69	99.02	98.95	95.45	98.12
Tibet	0.98	0.60	0.98	1.05	0.98	0.76
Other Countries	5.14	1.71	—	—	3.53	1.12

SOURCE: *Far Eastern Economic Review*, Vol. 35, March 16, 1962, p. 619.

Some trade was formerly carried on with Tibet, but the volume has dwindled since the Chinese occupation of the plateau. There is some *entrepôt* trade between India and Tibet through Nepal, but this, too, has declined considerably as a result of the India-China border dispute and political developments in Tibet. The direct commercial route between India and Lhasa lies through Sikkim, a shorter and better route than those through the passes of Nepal Himalaya. The limited India-Tibet trade therefore flows through Sikkim and Chumbi Valley; this route is now closed.

The projected Lhasa-Katmandu highway visualizes a rapid growth of trade between Tibet and Nepal in the future. Since trade between Tibet and Nepal has been limited in quantity to what the fleets of mules can carry, the highway is expected to facilitate an increase in the volume of trade. China has already prepared the blueprint for a railway connecting Lhasa with Peking; the proposed Lhasa-Katmandu highway will assume much more economic significance with the completion of the rail link. Many Nepalese take comfort in the thought that the road will lessen Nepal's dependence on India not only in trade and commerce, but also militarily.

In view of the predominantly agricultural character of the country's economy, imports from India are naturally concentrated on basic industrial products which are not made in Nepal. Cotton textile is the chief product, followed by cigarettes, consumption of which is quite high. Other significant imported commodities have been metal articles, hardware, kerosene, petrol, and cement. The principal articles of export from Nepal into India are agricultural products such as rice, mustard, and oil seeds. Raw jute has been an important export from the eastern Terai, though since 1952 the quantity has declined.

Trade between the United States and Nepal is almost nil. Those American consumer goods found in the Nepalese market are of Indian origin. Traditionally, whatever is imported into India flows freely into Nepal. This aspect of trade has been emphasized in the Indo-Nepal Treaty of Trade and Transit which came into force in November, 1960.

Most of Nepal's trade will remain confined to India in the future. The market for Indian goods can be affected only if this Himalayan kingdom starts importing from other countries. The possibility of Nepal doing so appears slight as it has little or no foreign exchange reserves. However, under the Indo-Nepal trade agreement of 1960, Nepal has the freedom to pursue its own trade with foreign countries. Indian exports to Nepal, which at present amount to about U.S. $50 million (250 million Rupees) annually, are increasing rapidly.

During the last ten years there has been a tremendous rise in imports—from about 80 million Rupees in 1949-1950 to about 290 million Rupees in 1959-1960—while exports have remained more or less constant with 125 million Rupees in 1949-1950 and 130 million Rupees in 1959-1960. These trends in Nepal's overall foreign trade, also applicable to trade with India, have produced an unfavorable trade balance.

DEVELOPMENT PROGRAM

A five-year development plan (1956-1957 to 1960-1961), calling for the expenditure of an estimated $69 million, was launched by the government of Nepal in 1956. The improvement of transportation and communication facilities accounted for nearly one-third of the total expenditure in the development plan. Further, agricultural improvement, resource surveys, the training of technical and administrative personnel, and the construction of schools and hospitals received priority in the five-year plan.

In July, 1961, at the end of the first five-year plan period, the major development projects remained uncompleted because of the grave shortage of investment capital. Ordinarily, about 85 per cent of Nepal's annual development expenditure has come from foreign aid. In 1959-1960 the dependence on foreign aid was 87 per cent, and in the following year it was as high as 94 per cent, reflecting a serious economic crisis in Nepal's struggle to develop a modern economy. During 1961-1962 Nepalese financial reserves were reported to be so low that funds had to be juggled from one ministry to another to keep the government in operation.[23] Further lack of resources forced the government to declare 1961-1962 as a planless year.

Nepal's second development plan, covering a three-year period, started in July, 1962. This plan has three main objectives: (1) agriculture and village development; (2) the expansion of facilities for transport, communications, and power; and (3) improvements

[23] Grimes, Paul, "Nepalese Facing Economic Crisis," *New York Times,* January 28, 1962, p. 22.

in health and education services. Some of the specific projects included in the plan are the east-west road to link Nepal's eastern and western borders through the southern foothills region; the Katmandu-Lhasa highway under Chinese aid; hydroelectric projects such as the Trisuli (Nepal's biggest under Indian aid) and the much smaller Panauti (under Soviet aid); airfields at Mustang and Jumla, both near the Tibet border; the paper and cement plans under Chinese aid; and the sugar and cigarette factories with Soviet aid. Out of a total plan outlay of about $97 million, Nepal expects to secure $60 million from foreign aid. India has promised $40 million in aid for Nepal's second development plan. The other foreign aid missions are being requested to make their assistance to Nepal's second plan.

The benefits envisaged at the end of the Second Plan (1965) are an increase of 200,000 tons of grain, 86,000 tons of jute, 9,000 tons of sugar, 25,000 kilowatt hours of power, irrigation facilities for 162,000 acres, four airports and thirty landing strips, 1,000 miles of road, 900 telephone lines, 26 post offices, primary education for 60,000 children, three hospitals totaling 360 beds, and ten health centers.

So far Nepal's biggest development aid benefactors are India and the United States, which have contributed the equivalent of about $60,000,000 and $51,000,000 respectively. Nepal has been unsuccessful in securing dollar loans from the United States because of her inability to repay them. It has so few American dollars and English pounds sterling to buy capital goods needed in economic development that it places high value on the British salaries and pensions paid to Gurkha troops who serve in or have retired from the British army.

In April, 1962, the United States made available a sum of $3.6 million for development purposes during the American fiscal year ending June, 1962. This additional assistance is supported by $11.2 million equivalent in Nepalese currency already made available by the United States earlier in the fiscal year. The combined amount represents the largest grant made available to Nepal by the United States for development purposes in any single year since the be ginning of American aid in 1952. In close alignment with Nepal's development planning, the United States aid is now concentrated in a small number of fields. This policy resulted from the realization that American aid was being provided in so many different fields that it was not possible to provide maximum benefit in all fields. Three major considerations have guided the selection of projects for American aid; Nepal's development priorities; the kind of projects expected to make significant impact within a reasonable period of time; and the type of projects to which the United States is particularly qualified to contribute. The sectors chosen for primary emphasis under the American aid program in 1962 are as follows: education and training in all professional fields for the maximum development of Nepal's most important resource—its people; government management and institutional development to permit most effective use of limited resources, domestic and foreign; development of roads, aviation, suspension bridges, and cableways; financial institutions, including both the Nepal Industrial Development Corporation and the expanded rural credit facilities; and forest development—both forestry and forest products.

Nepal has received the equivalent of $21.6 million in aid from Communist China, and grants totaling 30 million rubles from the Soviet Union for various development projects. In 1961 China announced that she would contribute more economic aid in addition to a grant equivalent to $9,800,000 for the construction of the Lhasa-Katmandu highway.

From the pattern of development assistance to Nepal so far, it is clear that while India and the United States have been extending substantial economic assistance, largely directed to basic agricultural and transport development, China and Russia have chosen to aid chiefly in the kingdom's industrialization. In general, the industrial projects such as the building of a cigarette factory or a sugar mill, financed by aid from the Sino-Soviet Bloc, do not represent fundamental improvements in the Nepalese economy, but they have considerable propaganda value for Communist nations.

The Israeli firm of Solel Boneh has provided Nepal with capital to set up the National Construction Company which will be in charge of construction works in the public sector, including road building. Japan has promised technical assistance in regard to small-scale industries, and West Germany plans to build a technical institute in Katmandu.

NEPAL: EXTERNAL RELATIONS

Although the geographic position of Nepal has influenced its internal political development, even greater importance can be attached to this same factor as an influencing element in external political relations. The geographic isolation of the country ended in 1950 with the opening of the air route linking Katmandu with India. The communication ties, coupled with Nepal's admission to the United Nations and the opening of the American, Russian, and Chinese embassies during the last decade, has witnessed an outstanding change in the world relations of Nepal. Because of its strategic location on the fringe of the Communist empire, Nepal has become part of the Free World's first line of defense against Communist expansion. Today more and more countries are establishing diplomatic relations with strategic Nepal. In early 1961 there were 27 diplomatic missions in Katmandu.

NEPAL, CHINA, AND THE INTERNATIONAL COMMUNIST MOVEMENT

The interests of China in Nepal can be said to be mainly concerned with Communist strategy in South Asia. Despite Nepal's concern about events in Tibet, and despite small provocations along the border, which included the killing of a Nepalese officer in June, 1960, by Chinese troops, the Nepalese government's stated intention of following a policy of friendship with Communist China remains unchanged. But underneath, the suspicion is growing that Nepal may be on China's timetable for Communist infiltration and subversion during the next five years.

Nepal's royal government has no illusions about the Chinese. Nepalese leaders have strongly criticized India for failing clearly to condemn Chinese actions in Tibet. However, some of the considerations that kept India quiet in 1950 and during the Lhasa uprising of 1959 apply even more strongly to Nepal. Its very weakness and backwardness seem to dictate neutrality and acceptance of aid from both neighbors, China and India.

Nepal has struggled hard to get along well with China, but the weight of troops building up in Tibet has made this increasingly difficult. The Chinese have crossed the border many times, collecting firewood and sometimes taxes, surveying, and occasionally warning Bhutia villagers (Nepali mountaineers of Tibetan origin) that they belong to Tibet and will someday come under its campus. The Nepalese government has ignored, and occasionally denied, these reports despite the alarm raised by responsible leaders about such incidents. However, when the Chinese claimed the southern slopes of Mount Everest, there were emotional outcries from the Nepalese public. The greatest claim to fame of the Nepalese is their mountains and especially their possession of the highest summit in the world. Even when China denied having claimed the southern slopes of Mount Everest, the government blundered into assertions that the entire peak belonged to Nepal while denying any claim to the northern slopes. The former prime minister ended up with the remarkable argument that ownership of the peak depended on which way it "inclined"; he assumed that it sloped towards Nepal because that was the only direction from which it had been climbed. Since the Chinese claim to have climbed it from their side also, the question of Everest was left up in the clouds that shroud it. On the maps accompanying the Sino-Nepalese boundary agreement of 1961, Mount Everest is shown on the Nepal-Tibet border.

Nepal had five other, less spectacular, border disputes with China. These disputes have been solved in the 1961 boundary agreement. Nepal has accepted the Chinese proposal (rejected by India in her border dispute) to withdraw armed patrols 20 kilometers from the boundary. On her part, Nepal had little to withdraw, but in some frontier villages Gurkha ex-servicemen were given small arms in order to avoid leaving a vacuum. The Chinese on their side never withdrew the considerable forces they had accumulated at the ends of the roads that are being built up to many of the 17 passes into

Nepal. To do so would have left a sanctuary for Tibetan resistance, which has become increasingly active in western Tibet as Chinese suppression tightens in the east.

A shortage of personnel has kept the Nepalese government from sending its officers into remote folds of the Great Himalaya facing Tibet, but now it plans to have regular visits made to any place where herdsmen or salt collectors can go. More radio posts have been established, and attempts are being made to accelerate the present mule-speed reports from some areas. Finally, aware of the Communist threat, Nepalese troops are being moved, by foot, into frontier areas just behind the demilitarized zone. The purpose of all this is not so much to bolster defences as to reassure the population, which became panicky in the Mustang area and has long been nervous in other border regions. In any case, Nepal's 10,000-man army could do little against Chinese aggression. To call home the 10,000 Gurkhas in the British army and 21,000 in the Indian army, as suggested by some Nepalese leaders in 1960, would not solve the problem, nor would the plan to use the many still youthful Gurkha ex-servicemen who live up in the mountains.

Nepalese leaders feel that the real defense of the country lies in the chain of events that they presume—and hope China recognizes— would be touched off by a Communist attack on Nepal. India has declared that any aggression against Nepal would be aggression against India, giving Nepal all the advantages of a military alliance without the liabilities of abandoning neutrality. Dependence on India for protection against Chinese Communist threats, nevertheless, poses problems for Nepal. Until 1958 India manned check posts on Nepal's Tibetan border, and although Nepalese officers are now in command, several Indians remain at these posts. Officially, they are radio operators and technicians, but in addition to sending coded radio reports for the Nepalese, it is said that the Indians also report directly to the huge Indian embassy in Katmandu, thus creating an Indian intelligence system within Nepal. Although the Nepal government accepts Indian intelligence as a necessary part of the defense of the Himalaya, the small, vigorous Communist party of Nepal does not. The Nepalese Communists use anti-Indian propaganda to divert public attention from their own subversive acts and China's atrocities in Tibet. The royal government has launched a campaign to cut the ground from under Communist propaganda, but the job is made difficult by the support for the local Communists coming from the new Soviet embassy and a Chinese aid mission.[24] In the summer of 1960, the government suggested, but did not formally request, the departure of a Russian first secretary who visited Communist party headquarters.

During 1960-1961 Communist strength in Nepal has steadily grown.[25] In early 1962 the kingdom appeared to be growing increasingly vulnerable to a Communist threat that could imperil the security of all southern Asia. Part of the force and inspiration of Communism in Nepal is endemic and reflects local injustice; but few can deny the close relationship between the Nepalese Communist Party and the international Communist movement which aspires to absorb Nepal, just as it aspires to absorb every other nation. Nepal's Communist party is strong enough to defy the government machinery. While the top political leaders of other parties are in jail, the government has been able to track down only 3 of the 17 principal Communist leaders. Nepal's top-ranking Communists are all within the country and, unlike leaders of other parties, have not gone over to India since the large-scale political arrests of December, 1960. Though the Communist party was not very successful in the 1959 general election, during the past two years their membership has increased substantially. At the time of the 1959 elections, the membership of the Communist party was estimated at 6,000; in 1961 it was estimated at 10,000. In the Katmandu Valley, Pokhara, Dhankuta, Palpa, and Dang and in eastern Terai, the Communist party has entrenched itself. Politico-geographically, the significant fact is that the Nepalese Communists are anti-Indian and attempt to foster Communist China's expansion south of the Himalaya.

The future course of action of the Communists in Nepal seems uncertain. However, the suspension of democratic functions in

---

[24] *The Economist* (London), August 27, 1960, p. 815.

[25] "Report on Nepal," *The Statesman,* Calcutta, March 13, 1961, p. 6; "Red Threat Growing in Nepal," *New York Times,* January 27, 1962, p. 5.

December, 1960, has brought into sharp focus the role that Communists may play in their bid for power. For one thing, the ban on political activity has benefited the Communist party most, because it has an organization that can work most efficiently underground. The ban has made it easier for the Nepalese Communists to organize a "united front." For the time being the Communists are not against the monarchy in Nepal. The Communists have always been successful when there was a czar or a Chiang Kai-Shek, but not when democratic parties function. To assume power in the latter situation the Communists must cross two hurdles: democratic institutions and the ruler. Under the present circumstances in Nepal the hurdles have been reduced to one—the king. Communist China regards the period of suspension of the elected government as the most suitable time to help strengthen the internal organization of the Nepalese Communist Party so that in time they can overthrow the king and then take over the country.

One possible answer to the external Communist pressure from China and the internal pressure from the local Communists is an improvement in Nepal's defenses and her still primitive, feudal economy. However, the government is not even able to pay its financial share of the development program conducted with foreign aid; an urgently requested American grant of $15 million, 41 per cent of the budget, kept the basic programs of agricultural and educational improvement going in 1961. Bigger projects for road construction and irrigation works are behind schedule and cannot be completed with the money or in the time allotted for them. Nepal needs time to prepare against the Communist threat, particularly infiltration from Communist China. The local Communists are trying to win over the frustrated Nepalese youth and through them attempt to put pressure on the Nepalese leaders to criticize the government headed by King Mahendra, and finally to incite agitation on sectional issues such as regional and linguistic demands, whipping up discontent to create a situation in which the Communists can make their bid for control of the government. A few years ago Nepalese intellectuals believed that the Communists would allow them time to consolidate the nation. Now the responsible Nepalese leaders dedicated to keeping Nepal free from Communist rule are not so certain. Today the Communist party is a powerful underground force, and its dominant faction would not hesitate to accept Chinese support in the border regions.

King Mahendra professes a distaste for Communism. He has declared that he "never can imagine that the King and the Communists can go together." [26] Yet he has given the Communists broad opportunities for infiltration and subversion through his domestic and foreign policies. Political observers in Katmandu doubt that the king is adequately aware of the Communist threat or has the capacity to control it. During 1961-1962 King Mahendra strengthened Nepal's relations with Communist China. While India and China argued bitterly about 51,000 square miles of Himalayan territory, Nepal and China signed a border treaty. In October, 1961, the king agreed to let Communist China build a strategic highway from Katmandu to Tibet. In 1960 the Koirala government had turned down the proposal to build this highway. King Mahendra's foreign policy toward the Sino-Soviet bloc is a cause for special concern because in Nepal Communist expansionist aims conflict directly with the Free World's interest and security in South Asia.

NEPAL AND INDIA

If China's main interest in Nepal is the expansion of Communist influence, India's interest is economic and cultural as well as strategic. In a sense, Chinese penetration in Nepal Himalaya is merely designed to secure a stepping-stone to fresh expansion of their power in South Asia. But India is in a different geopolitical position as far as Nepal is concerned. Her geography and economic-cultural connections make essential the development of close contact with the Himalayan kingdom, not merely as an adjunct to her economy, but also as a strategic necessity. This position in turn involves the maintenance of political strength in order to prevent interference with or discrimination against her economic and political interests

[26] *New York Times,* January 20, 1962.

in Nepal. As Prime Minister Nehru put it in Parliament in December, 1950:

> Our interest in the internal conditions of Nepal has become still more acute and personal, because of the developments across our borders, to be frank, especially those in China and Tibet. Besides our sympathetic interest in Nepal, we were also interested in the security of our own country. From time immemorial, the Himalayas have provided us with a magnificent frontier. Of course, they are no longer as impassable as they used to be but are still fairly effective. The Himalayas lie mostly on the northern border of Nepal. We cannot allow that barrier to be penetrated because it is also the principal barrier to India. Therefore, much as we appreciate the independence of Nepal, we cannot allow anything to go wrong in Nepal or permit that barrier to be crossed or weakened, because that would be a risk to our own security.[27]

Achievement of the objective indicated by Nehru demands a subtle and imaginative Indian policy based on close understanding of the physical and human environment of Nepal, a policy sensitive to local developments. Unfortunately, this understanding has not yet been fully attained, and consequently Indo-Nepal relations have in recent years been somewhat strained.

Unlike Sikkim's and Bhutan's, Nepal's relations with India are complicated and delicate. A treaty (which, like the Indo-Sikkim treaty, was signed in 1950) provides for consultation between India and Nepal in the event of external threat to the independence or security of either of them. The nature of the Indian goal in Nepal —to protect Indian security through the development of a government capable of performing needed services and of carrying out needed reforms—has shown clearly in Indian policy during the last decade. In spite of pressing needs at home, Indian experts have been dispatched to Nepal to train an army and a civil service, to build schools and roads where almost none existed before. The financial efforts India is making in Nepal are shown by the fact that since 1950 India has spent millions of dollars in that country

---

[27] *Jawaharlal Nehru's Speeches, 1949-1953,* Ministry of Information and Broadcasting, Delhi, 1954, p. 176.

for development purposes. Undoubtedly, Indian aid in Nepal, involving calculations of high strategy, economic planning, and military aid programs, are designed to bring maximum returns for the expenditures. This aid is intended to build a shield to keep Chinese power contained north of the Great Himalaya. However, Nepalese politicians, suspicious of Indian imperialism, have frequently fulminated against India.

Extreme sensitivity to Indian domination generates strong anti-Indian feeling in Nepal. Because of the Indian criticism of the democratic setback in Nepal, the anti-Indian feeling ran high after the king's dismissal of elected government in December, 1960. The anti-Indian sentiment affords excellent propaganda for enemies of democracy and the Free World. The Indians point to the contemporary Chinese expansion and repeat India's desire to encourage democracy, to raise literacy, and to increase living standards of the people. Yet, in spite of the logic of the Indian viewpoint, the Nepalese adopt a skeptical approach. A Nepalese politician even warned Sikkim and Bhutan of Indian designs, asked them to free themselves from Indian interference, and called for a federation of Nepal, Sikkim, and Bhutan, under Nepal's leadership.

Several explanations can be offered for the existence of anti-Indian feeling in Nepal. To begin with, the Rana elements had been dissatisfied with India since 1950 because of its policy toward the incidents that led to the overthrow of the feudal government by the Rana family at that time. Second, the Nepalese public have suspected an Indian hand in making or breaking the successive cabinets which came into power since 1951. Third, the elected government of Koirala was accused by his opponents of having pro-Indian leanings; although the charge was far from true, it reinforced anti-Indian sentiment. Fourth, the occasional mismanagement of the huge Indian aid by Indian personnel and technicians led to further criticism of India. Finally, behind Nepal's anti-Indian feeling is the real fear of a larger nation dominating its economy and trade. More than 90 per cent of Nepal's foreign trade is controlled by the Indian business community.

The existence of anti-Indian feeling should not be overemphasized, however. Although no one can deny the anti-Indian sentiment in Katmandu Valley, the majority of the Hindi-speaking people of the Terai—nearly 60 per cent of the total population—are pro-Indian. In the mountain areas outside the Katmandu Valley, people generally follow a friendly policy toward India, while ex-army Gurkha soldiers stand by India. But strangely, the small anti-Indian feudal elements in Nepal feel that the Tibetan revolt against China and the subsequent influx of refugees from Communism was the result of a clash between India and China.

Further, both China and Russia have effective organizations in Katmandu to foment anti-Indian feeling, aimed to dislodge India from the dominant position she holds in Nepal and to bring the Himalayan country into their sphere of influence. For instance, Communist sympathizers assert that India is doing much less for Nepal than she could (though half the total foreign aid is from India and nearly 88 per cent of the nation's budget is dependent on foreign aid) and that the development projects undertaken by India could be finished in half the time. While the shortcomings of the Indian policy are exaggerated, few Nepalese talk of the massive Chinese Communist infiltration through organic relationship between the local political party and the international Communist movement. Responsible leaders in Nepal are aware that China is a great threat to Nepal's security and believe that, although friendship with China may be good, it should not be promoted at the cost of allowing local Communists to gain a strong position.

In recent years several factors have produced tension between India and Nepal. Most of the political and economic factors creating tension are relatively minor, but potentially they are capable of causing serious rifts. Significant among the political factors causing tension are the presence of the Indian military mission, started in 1952 to train and reorganize the Royal Nepal Army; the Indian radio operators on the 14 check posts on the northern border who are accused of spying; and the five Indian commercial attachés in South Nepal who are branded as "intelligence men." The presence of exiled Nepalese politicians in India who vociferously oppose King Mahendra's dismissal of parliamentary democracy is another source of Indo-Nepalese tension. According to the Nepalese government, the politicians in exile in India are responsible for the striking increase in rebel activity in the kingdom. King Mahendra himself has denounced these Nepalese leaders for directing guerrilla violence "from the sanctuary of a foreign power." In January, 1962, when an attempt was made to bomb his car, the king repeated the charge, saying "Some people from foreign soil are making improper efforts to disturb the peace in the country." [28] One Nepali newspaper (controlled by the government) accused India of seeking to "do a Cuba" on Nepal. India has, of course, never hidden its sympathies for democratic forces in Nepal. ("A setback to democracy" Nehru termed the December, 1960, *coup d'état* by the king). It has granted shelter to dismissed Nepalese politicians and, so far, has not imposed any curb on their political activity. But India has rejected Nepalese charges that guerrilla activity is being directed from Indian soil. As far as India's foreign policy toward Nepal is concerned, the important question is: Should India put its democratic ideals first, or its strategic national interests? In Nepal, India "faces a mild form of America's Cuban dilemma, whether to back friends against a disgruntled neighbour, or to placate him for fear of further estrangement."[29]

Among the economic factors, the recent Indo-Nepal trade treaty, which gives free trade rights to India, is a source of rift. Nepalese complain that free trade leading to a common market is advantageous only to industrially developed India. Further, since India doesn't pay in hard currency, free trade limits Nepal's foreign-exchange earning and makes her economically dependent on India. India, however, does not consider Nepal an export market since it earns no foreign exchange by selling in Nepal. Foreign goods meant for India's internal market, even goods with a large foreign exchange element like cars, usually enter Nepal without restriction.

The Indo-Nepal agreement on the utilization of Gandak waters for irrigation and power development is another source of vexation.

[28] *Times of India* (Delhi), January 24, 1962.
[29] "India's Dilemma in Nepal," *The Economist* (London), February 17, 1962, p. 624.

Although Nepal's sovereignty and territorial jurisdiction remain supreme, some Nepalese view the river agreement with suspicion and feel that it compromises the nation's sovereignty. The Gandak project envisages construction of a barrage[30] on the Indo-Nepal border with one end in Nepal and the other in the Bihar state of India. The two main projected canals on the western and eastern banks of the river also start within Nepalese and Indian territories, respectively. Of the two power stations with a capacity of 10,000 kilowatts each, one will be on the Nepalese and the other on the Indian side of the border.[31] The criticism persists despite the fact that the entire project is being financed by India, and Nepal will receive, free of cost, power supply and irrigation facilities for nearly 300,000 acres in the upper reaches of the Gandak.

The Indian aid program poses another problem. Although Indian aid is designed to enhance the stability and security of the kingdom, Nepalese often complain of "wastage" and sum up their dissatisfaction in the Indian effort by the term "no concrete results." The substantial financial efforts India is making in Nepal are shown by the fact that in 1960, India spent more than 36 million rupees in that country for development purposes and comparable expenditures have continued. The construction, maintenance, and repairs of roads, building of permanent runways and an air terminal at Katmandu, minor irrigation and water supply schemes, aerial surveys and mapping, and help in the development of Tribhuvana University of Katmandu are among the principal works undertaken by India. Six irrigation schemes, including the important Tika-Bhairab Canal and the Phewatal irrigation project in Pokhara Valley, and 14 drinking-water supply schemes have already been completed with Indian aid, and in 1962 India provided additional funds for a basic water supply and power development in the kingdom.[32] Under an agreement signed in November, 1961, Nepal will receive substantial aid

[30] In geographic usage, a barrage is an artificial barrier or obstruction placed in a river to divert it into a channel for irrigation, navigation, etc.

[31] "Agreement on Gandak Project," *Foreign Affairs Record,* Vol. V, No. 12, December, 1959, New Delhi, Ministry of External Affairs, pp. 493-494.

[32] *Far Eastern Economic Review,* Vol. 35, February 22, 1962, p. 397.

from India for undertaking important geological investigations. Further, Indian economic aid provides for the establishment of an Institute of Forestry at Hitaura in Central Nepal. The large Trisuli hydroelectric power project northwest of Katmandu Valley is being constructed with Indian aid.

India announced a substantial aid program in 1962 to provide basic amenities for the capital city of Katmandu. Because of the rapid growth of Katmandu water supply, lighting and power needs have grown considerably. Indian aid will augment Katmandu's water supply to five million gallons per day; and new power stations are expected to bolster the deteriorating power-supply position in the capital. Further, under the new aid program India will construct a general post office building in Katmandu and help in improving the postal service in the capital. Katmandu's maternity home and child welfare center will be assisted by construction of several needed buildings and provision of new equipment. India will construct a modern and well-equipped national archives building in Katmandu. Further, Indian aid provides for the construction of a science block, a library building, student's dormitories, and staff quarters for the Tribhuvana University on its new campus.

Under the Intensive Katmandu Valley Development Scheme, Patan (one of the three towns of Katmandu Valley) will get multi-sided development which includes the expansion and development of the hospital, construction of a high school, a new post office, and a tourist bureau. The proposed industrial estate at Patan, which will be constructed with Indian aid, will provide a new and more fruitful outlet for skills of the craftsmen of the valley.

As a part of the development assistance India has provided the government of Nepal not only financial aid, but also technical personnel of the needed categories, even though they are in short supply in India itself. In 1962 over 200 qualified Indian technical personnel were working in the kingdom. Further, the technical advice and guidance of the highest Indian government agencies like the Central Water and Power Commission, Survey of India, and Geological Survey of India are also available to Nepal for planning and execution of development projects. Above all, India has provided during the last ten years training for more than 1,500 Nepalese personnel in different institutions in India to assist in the implementation of development plans.

In addition to the general cost of development projects, India, unlike China and the Soviet Union, also bears the "local costs" of all the projects. On projects sponsored by other governments, Nepal has found it difficult to meet these local costs, which involve purchase of land, construction of approach roads to sites, and labor. These costs vary between 20 and 70 per cent of the total cost of the development projects. India and the United States are the only foreign governments that pay for the "local costs" of their projects.

Despite India's massive development aid and her keen interest in the growth of an economically and politically stable nation, xenophobia against India continues in Nepal. This distrust or fear has led Nepal to assert her political independence even by carrying the friendship of countries with which India is at odds. For example, the king of Nepal announced visits to Pakistan and China during the fall of 1961. These visits, especially his Pakistan visit, are regarded in India with great concern. Further, in October, 1961, Nepal and Communist China signed an agreement for the construction of a motor road between Katmandu and Lhasa. This road-building agreement has disturbed India. Nepal insists that "the agreement to build the Katmandu-Lhasa road with Chinese aid did not involve any strategy nor did it constitute a danger to anyone, least of all to India." [33] India, however, views it in purely strategic terms (probably rightly, in view of the similar agreement recently concluded by the Chinese with the Pathet Lao). The new road will not only open Nepal to Chinese penetration, but will pose a direct military threat to India, the more so because there is already a road link between Katmandu and India.

As far as the solution of the major Indo-Nepal problems are concerned, there was little gain from the talks between the Nepalese king and the Indian prime minister in April 1962. King Mahendra was not satisfied with Nehru's assurance that, while freedom of expression was permitted in India for the exiled Nepalese leaders, the

[33] *Times of India,* November 30, 1961.

Indian government would not allow unlawful political agitation against the king's regime from the Indian territory. Nehru implied that in continuation of its policies, India would take steps to prevent armed subversion in Nepal from the Indian territory, but constitutional agitation from India for democratic government in Nepal would not be curbed. Likewise, King Mahendra's explanation that the projected Katmandu-Lhasa road, to be built with Chinese aid, was needed for commercial purposes failed to satisfy the prime minister. Burdened with a dispute with China on her northern borders, India remains displeased over Nepal's treaty with China under which the Katmandu-Lhasa highway is to be built.

However, irrespective of Nepal's actions and drift towards a policy of neutralism between India and China, geographic proximity, economic ties, and cultural affinities will keep India's influence dominant in the Himalayan kingdom.

NEPAL AND THE UNITED STATES

In attempting to evaluate the role of the United States in Nepal, a major consideration is the kingdom's geographical location with relation to Communist Asia. Although the United States established first formal relations with Nepal as early as April 1947,[34] it was not until the 1950 advance of Communist China in Tibet that political contacts became closer. The Communist occupation of Tibet greatly increased the strategic value of Nepal to the Free World, and in 1951 American economic aid under the Point Four Program was extended to enhance Nepal's security. Since 1952 a United States Operations Mission (USOM) has been functioning in Katmandu to supervise and administer economic aid. The total American aid until the end of June 1961 amounted to nearly $51,000,000, in addition to 400,000 in Indian currency from the Development Loan Fund. The United States has agreed to provide $4,225,270 in aid during 1961-1962. In 1961 a U.S. Educational Foundation was set up in Katmandu to provide for cultural and educational exchanges.

The American goal in Nepal is to help build a stable economy

[34] U. S. Department of State, *The Kingdom of Nepal,* Dept. of State Publication 6953, Washington, D.C., 1960, p. 12.

strong enough to resist and combat Communist pressures at home and from abroad. In this respect the United States' interest in Nepal parallels those of India. Moreover, the foreign aid operations of the United States and India in Nepal offer an unusual example of international cooperation. Technical assistance projects under the American Aid Program are planned in consultation with Indian officials. In such enterprises as road building, the development of air transport, and health and education services, there is a joint Indian-American participation. For example, Indians with Nepalese help are building landing strips, and Americans are installing navigational aids at the new airfields.

The first projects undertaken with USOM cooperation included village development, agriculture, mineral resource surveys, and the irrigation schemes (on Sirsia, Bara District, and Tilawee River, Parsa District) in eastern Terai. In 1954 education, malaria control, and local health services were added to the list of projects financed by the United States. During the same year the United States contributed to flood relief efforts in Nepal. The equipment and supplies provided during the flood emergency assistance afforded an opportunity to undertake cooperative work in the multipurpose development of the Rapti Valley in Central Inner Terai. The Rapti Valley Development Project, completed in 1961, represents by far the most important and impressive American aid to Nepal. The Rapti Valley, now popularly called the "American" valley, was a backward, sparsely settled, malarial region, used by the Rana rulers for a few months of hunting each year. United States aid eradicated malaria through an intensive DDT-spraying program, and built an all-weather road in the valley. The new road and the anti-malaria campaign have now opened new land in the valley for settlement of thousands of homeless and landless Nepalese farmers. The western area of the Rapti Valley was opened for settlement in 1961 with the completion of the American-built ferry across the Narayani River, which provides a link with the trail leading westward to Bhairawa (Majhkhanda district) in the midwestern Terai.

Since 1955 American aid has greatly expanded—as much as a

nation with the economic and administrative structure of Nepal can profitably absorb with maximum advantage. The important American aid programs being carried out now include development of highways, roadways, telecommunications, suspension bridges, aviation, and the Industrial Development Corporation. By the middle of 1963, a 28-mile aerial ropeway, costing over $3,000,000, to haul 25 tons of freight an hour in buckets over the mountains between Katmandu and Terai will be completed. Further, the United States is constructing roads between jungle towns that now are linked to Katmandu only by runners, who take as long as 22 days to reach the more remote valleys.

A major American project is the establishment of an improved telephone system within Katmandu, a radio-telephone network extending to all the districts of Nepal and also to New Delhi and Calcutta in India. An American helicopter, the first in Nepal, carries telecommunications equipment to far-off and inaccessible places in order to connect them with the capital. The telecommunications project, like the regional roads, is a tripartite effort in which Nepal, the United States, and India are cooperating. In April, 1962, Nepal's first automatic telephone exchange, built by the United States, was completed at a cost of $500,000 in American aid.

In total amount, the American aid now ranks as high as the Indian aid in Nepal. Undoubtedly, the United States has been a leader in the spending race in Nepal by pouring in over $50,000,000 —more than the total income of the Nepalese government. But the program, like the Indian aid, has not aroused great local enthusiasm for America. Most of the American aid has gone into projects far from the densely populated Katmandu Valley, such as in the development of malarial Rapti Valley, and in the remote Pokhara Valley where conditions were so backward until a few years ago that the first wheel anybody ever saw was on an airplane bringing in supplies. In contrast to the substantial American and Indian aid projects, which are building the basic economic foundations of Nepal in the fields of agriculture and transportation, meager economic aid from Communist China and the Soviet Union is being spent on minor projects in and around the Katmandu Valley. The

Communist aid projects are designed to yield maximum propaganda and publicity dividends. In addition, the Communists have made token gifts from time to time. For example, in 1957 Red Chinese Premier Chou En-Lai donated $4,000 for a Buddhist shrine in Katmandu. This small gift from Communist China made such a big splash in Nepal that an American foreign aid official in Katmandu who supervised the expenditure of millions of United States dollars for development projects declared in exasperation: "I think we should cut out everything else and give them money to build the biggest damned tower you ever saw, right in the middle of Katmandu. It won't mean anything, but they'll see it and talk about it. Maybe they'll even begin to worship it!"

It is hard to convince anti-Indian and anti-American politicians and leaders in Katmandu of the significant contribution of American aid to Nepal's economy. The presence of a group of nearly 50 American technicians and administrators and their families "living in the former Rana palaces in luxury (according to Nepalese standards), spending evenings at the bar of the International Club with the third prince or some Rana playboy, engenders criticism from the Nepalese politicians" [35] and obscures the value of United States efforts even, at times, among the better-informed Nepalese citizens.

NEPAL AND THE SOVIET UNION

The Soviet Union's overtures of friendship have supplemented Chinese Communist propaganda in Nepal. In the summer of 1958 the king of Nepal paid an official visit to the U.S.S.R. following the presentation of credentials by the Soviet ambassador in 1957. A Russian embassy was opened in Katmandu in 1959. The Soviet Union has agreed to provide the equivalent of $7.54 million in rubles, which will be used to construct a 50-bed hospital, a small sugar factory, a hydroelectric plant, and a saw mill. In addition, the Soviet Union has promised to make a survey for an east-west highway across the country. The Russian experts, who began their job in the fall of 1959, have completed aerial and ground surveys for

[35] *The Wall Street Journal,* May 26, 1958.

the alignment of this road. Work on other Russian projects has been delayed because of Nepal's inability to meet the local costs.[36]

The newly formed State Trading Corporation of Nepal announced in April, 1962, that sale proceeds of consumer goods received from China and the Soviet Union as part of the foreign aid will be utilized to meet the local costs of projects under aid from the Communist countries. In June, 1962, Nepal's Commerce Department revealed plans to bring large areas of land in the Terai districts of Bara, Parsa, and Rautahat under sugar-cane cultivation to supply the demands of the proposed sugar factory to be constructed in Birganj under Soviet aid. Also, Russian tobacco is being grown on an experimental basis near Janakpur, in eastern Terai, where the proposed Soviet-aided cigarette factory is to be constructed.

In the near future it seems unlikely that the U.S.S.R. will push forward too hard in Nepal. But, as one of the two major world powers, Russia obviously has global interests, particularly in the Himalayan region which lies adjacent to the Communist imperial order. In Nepal the Soviets will continue their long-range plan of infiltration to force social revolution favorable to the U.S.S.R. The Soviet Union has recently been sending Russian-made consumption goods such as watches, bicycles, and clothes in ever-increasing quantities. These sell at extremely low prices and constitute a powerful weapon of Communist propaganda. In 1961 Nepal and the Soviet Union signed a two-year cultural agreement to provide for greater contacts through the exchange of artists, writers, teachers, and journalists. These cultural exchanges furnish the Soviets strategic advantage in critical areas by creating a condition for social change leading to the Russian goal of world Communism.

NEPAL AND BRITAIN

Nepal's foreign relations with Britain date back to the eighteenth century, but formal relations were not established until 1815, when Nepal was forced to accept a British Resident officer at Katmandu. From 1815 to 1947, the British government in India completely

[36] *New York Times,* May 21, 1961; January 28, 1962.

dominated the Rana rulers and kept Nepal's external contacts strictly limited to Britain. The imperial policy kept Nepal an isolated buffer kingdom, with only formal independence, under the British sphere of influence in order to prevent the extension of Chinese influence from Tibet.

Since the withdrawal of British power from India in 1947, the principal interest of the United Kingdom in Nepal has been the retention of the right to recruit Gurkha soldiers for the British army in Southeast Asia. Under a 1947 agreement, Britain continued to recruit up to 12 battalions of Gurkhas and maintained recruitment depots in Uttar Pradesh in India, but in 1952 India withdrew Britain's privilege of recruiting Gurkhas in Indian territory. A new agreement, therefore, was signed with Nepal in 1953, permitting Britain to operate recruitment depots near Jaleshwar and Biratnagar in the Terai.

Because of popular Nepalese sentiment against recruitment of Gurkhas, the 1953 agreement is subject to termination at any time, although fighting manpower is still Nepal's most profitable export. The rise of nationalism is a factor in the present sentiment against the mercenaries. Educated Nepalese today are not flattered when a foreign visitor recalls the gallantry of Gurkha regiments in two World Wars. They appear to regard it as faintly disreputable that so many thousands of their countrymen found their livelihood fighting distant wars under alien flags. During the 1959 election campaign the Communist party made a public issue of Gurkha recruitment, contending that it was an affront to Nepalese dignity for Gurkha regiments to do the "dirty work" of "foreign imperialists." Other political parties ignored the issue, but agreed that Nepalese should not be allowed to hire themselves out as fighting men. However, they conceded that until Nepal could provide jobs at home for these men, nothing would be gained by forbidding further recruitment.

Nepal's own army of 10,000 men is too small to absorb the 25,000 Gurkhas serving abroad (15,000 men in the Indian army and 10,000 men in the British army). The pensions they send to their families while on active duty have long been Nepal's steadiest source of foreign exchange and a significant contribution to its national income. As a concession to the rising sentiment in Nepal, the United Kingdom is now somewhat close-mouthed about her recruiting activities, and the Gurkha tradition of soldiering in foreign armies appears to be on the way out.

NEPAL AND PAKISTAN

In January 1963 Pakistan and Nepal entered into an agreement granting each the right to tranship goods across the other's borders to "third countries." The third country is obviously China, and the route is the road from Lhasa to Katmandu that the Chinese are building. The agreement on transit was followed by another to establish scheduled air service between Katmandu and Dacca. These agreements have considerable political significance and are a result of Nepal's desire to establish a more independent position and Pakistan's goal of achieving stronger bargaining power in her negotiations over Kashmir. In the long run the national interest of Nepal and Pakistan will hardly be served by the new pacts. They tend to strengthen Communist China and to open the entire Indian subcontinent, of which Nepal and Pakistan are important parts, to further Chinese Communist incursions. Certainly Pakistan's recent agreement to cede to China more than 2,000 square miles of strategic borderland in Kashmir Himalaya has ruled out, for the present, hopes for a Kashmir settlement. In the final analysis both Nepal and Pakistan lose more than they gain—and the whole of South Asia may share in their losses.

V

The Balance of Power
in the Himalaya

> ". . . the imperialist States have taken away many Chinese dependent States and a part of her territories. Japan took away Korea, Taiwan and Ryuku islands . . . ; England seized Burma, Bhutan, Nepal . . . ; France occupied Annam . . ."
> —MAO TSE-TUNG in *Chinese Revolution and the Chinese Communist Party*

> From time immemorial, the Himalayas have provided us with a magnificent frontier. Of course, they are no longer as impassable as they used to be but are still fairly effective. . . . We cannot allow that barrier to be penetrated . . . , to be crossed or weakened, because that would be a risk to our own security.
> —JAWAHARLAL NEHRU in a speech before the Indian Parliament

THE Chinese invasion of Indian territory in October, 1962, brought into sharp focus the question of the future of the three Himalayan nations. In that hostile maneuver China demonstrated her apparent intention of gaining mastery over the approaches to northern India and establishing herself as the dominant political power of Asia.[1]

Resort to force came after a two-year period of diplomatic successes in which China cleverly estranged Nepal from her traditional ties to her southern neighbor and successfully posed as a friend of all bordering countries with the exception of her rival, India. This development occurred at a time when disclosures of economic distress and of agricultural failures threatened to do irreparable

[1] Trumbull, R., "Behind India-China Dispute: Leadership of Asia," *New York Times,* October 28, 1962, p. E7.

135

damage to Chinese prestige in Asia, a time when Communist Chinese achievements were seen to suffer in comparison with those of democratic India. Posing as the good neighbor, China settled her boundary disputes with Burma and Nepal on terms favorable to those countries. She also made overtures to Pakistan and did not aggressively pursue her demands upon Sikkim and Bhutan. She thus gained a diplomatic advantage and from a geopolitical standpoint effectively isolated India from its neighbors.

Through diplomacy China has entrenched herself in the Himalayan region. Nepalese-Chinese relations continue to reach higher levels of cordiality as of the beginning of 1963. Boundary pillars have been erected along the border of Nepal and Tibet; preliminary talks for a trade treaty have beeen completed; a detailed survey for the Katmandu-Lhasa highway is under way; and Chinese aid projects are making slow but steady progress. Perhaps of greater importance than any of the foregoing is the agreement on choice of nationality and trans-frontier cultivation and pasturing which affect the people along the Nepalese-Tibetan border. Communist influence is also receiving a boost from Russian and Chinese "aid" products which are "lent" to Nepal. These products, cars, motorcycles, watches, radios, pens, and other consumer goods sell on the Nepalese market at comparatively low prices.

King Mahendra wants to be recognized as the focal point of power in Nepal; his supremacy has been fully recognized by Communist China. The king wants India also to give unconditional support to his "direct rule," which over the long run goes counter to Indian support for democratic rule in the country. India's dilemma is China's opportunity. The establishment of closer relations with China and Pakistan and the reduction of India's influence in Nepal no doubt is a policy that gains King Mahendra support from anti-Indian Nepalese politicians.

False allegations of Indian assistance to rebels opposed to the royal regime strengthens King Mahendra's position, partly clouding the issue of internal resistance to royal rule. In November, 1962, Subarna Shumshere, acting president of the outlawed Nepalese Congress party, announced the temporary suspension of the rebel movement in Nepal in view of Chinese Communist aggression against India. One reason for suspending the movement, according to Mr. Shumshere, was to give King Mahendra an opportunity for second thoughts on his soft policy toward Communist China. Rebel leaders feared that a continuation of the movement might encourage the 40,000 Chinese soldiers massed along Nepal's northern border to move into the kingdom in accordance with the promise of armed assistance made to the King by Marshall Chen Yi, Chinese Foreign Minister. Nepal might yet learn, as has India, that trustful coexistence with Communist China can be a costly policy.

The capture of Towang, a few miles northeast of Bhutan, by the Chinese in October, 1962, has directly endangered Bhutan. It is completely separated from India by a high mountain range which can be crossed only by the Se Pass, at an altitude of about 10,000 feet. From Towang, on the other hand, a broad and easily accessible valley leads to Bhutan. In case of the extension of the India-China War, China may use India's obligation to maintain the territorial integrity of Bhutan as a pretext to invade the kingdom. China has warned Bhutan against the entry of Indian troops for the defense of the Himalayan kingdom.

The weight of the Chinese invasion has also been felt in neighboring Sikkim. The most dangerous spot potentially is the Chumbi Valley, a dagger-like slice of Tibetan territory between Sikkim and Bhutan. If the Chinese decide on an all-out war against India, they could strike southward from the valley. An advance of less than 80 miles would sever a vital Indian land corridor and cut off Sikkim, Bhutan, part of West Bengal, and all of Assam and the North East Frontier Agency from land access to the rest of India. The exchange of the Chinese-occupied Aksai Chin area of Ladakh for the Chumbi Valley has been suggested by a well-known Indian[2] in order to save the prestige of both sides and achieve strategic balance. From the Indian point of view the exchange would have the advantage of offering a concrete demonstration of China's ultimate intentions as far as the invasion of India is con-

[2] Rangaswami, K., *The Hindu Weekly Review* (Madras), July 30, 1962, p. 10.

cerned. It seems the Chinese would scarcely relinquish the Chumbi Valley if they have even the remote intention of invading India.

In assessing the future pattern of the balance of power in the Himalaya, the political aims of China and the extent to which they may be integrated with those of the Soviet Union are clearly the determining factor. However, strategic policy is a blend of aims and capabilities, each reacting upon the other, and the relative military resources of India and China are an important element in the assessment.

During the 1950's, when the Atlantic allies were closing ranks against the Communist military power which they saw threatening the free nations of Europe and Asia, India's government emerged as the most vocal spokesman for the peaceful intentions of Communist China. Western nations, preoccupied with evidence of Communist China's expansionist aims and bad faith, detected folly in India's policy toward China. When Chinese troops marched into Tibet in 1950, India urged the United Nations to drop the Tibetan complaint. In 1954, in an Indian-Chinese agreement on Tibet, India voluntarily relinquished the extraterritorial privileges taken over from the British and formally affirmed Chinese rule over Tibet. With that the Indian government's policy not only furthered Communist enslavement of Tibet, but also endangered the security of the Himalayan kingdoms.

When the border dispute broke out in 1959, abruptly ending friendly relations between India and China, based on the principles of trustful co-existence that were first framed in the 1954 Tibet agreement, the Indian government leaned heavily on the Soviet Union for support. The ideological controversy that was carried on openly as well as secretly in the Communist Bloc encouraged the Indian government to cling to its illusion that the Soviet Union would give the protection they needed against the Chinese threat in the Himalaya. But when the skirmishes along the Himalayan border turned into an undeclared war in October-November, 1962, the Soviet Union did not rise to India's defense.

China's military power is overwhelmingly greater than India's. Based upon a population of over 600,000,000, the People's Liberation Army is the largest in the world. The standing army alone is believed to number 2,500,000. Behind this considerable force, which many Chinese military planners regard as a small peacetime army, are the reserves—the "human sea" of militia which Mao Tse-tung has been developing since 1958. By comparison India does not possess adequate military strength. The present strength of the Indian Army is about 500,000 out of a total population of about 450,000,000. The number of effectively trained militia reserves is about 20,000.

The topography favors the attacker, who is advancing from the Tibetan plateau down the steep slopes of the Himalaya. Although India has been improving strategic communications in the Himalayan area since 1959-1960, the Chinese have been building roads and airfields since they invaded Tibet and have a more comprehensive logistic structure.[3]

Without doubt, India made serious mistakes in formulating its policy toward Communist China. In the purely military sphere, there seems little doubt that the defenses of the Himalayan region would be in better shape today if the danger of invasion from China had been frankly faced at an earlier stage. The eventual geostrategic pattern in the Himalaya will depend on the extent to which India can count on outside help. Britain and the United States have become identified with the conflict to the extent of providing small arms; but if the Chinese are intent upon major aggression in the Himalaya, much more than that will be needed to enable India to offer serious resistance.

The Himalayan kingdoms constitute a critical sector of the Free World's ceaseless struggle against Communist challenge. To Communist China, the high plateau of Tibet is like the palm of the hand with Ladakh, Nepal, Sikkim, Bhutan, and North East Frontier Agency as the five fingers. China has the palm under its control; now it wants the strategic five fingers without which the palm is not very useful. The leaders of Himalasia are acutely aware of the significant position their kingdoms occupy in South Asia between the Free and Communist Worlds. They are pushing

[3] Baldwin, Hanson W., "Mountain War in India" and "Measuring the Armies," *New York Times,* October 27, 1962, p. 2, and November 20, 1962, p. 4.

change, reform, and development as rapidly as they can, convinced that speed is of the essence if their archaic kingdoms are to preserve their independence in the swirling currents of the global conflict between the rival democratic and totalitarian systems. In Nepal, King Mahendra takes economic aid from both the East and West; here is a most fascinating example of Indian-American and Russian-Chinese aid programs in intense competition to influence the Nepalese. In Sikkim and Bhutan can be seen the orderly economic development under the Indian aid program, without undesirable East-West competition. Our over-all conclusion is that, for all its mistakes and deficiencies, the Free World (principally India and the United States) is holding its own, and more, in comparison with Communist China and the Soviet Union in the vital Himalayan kingdoms.

Geopolitically, China's successful Himalayan attack has resulted in answers to at least three questions that cannot fail to have an impact on Indo-Himalaysian relations. First, the Himalayan barrier *can* be breached by a determined invader; second, the Indian people can and will rise to an emergency with unity and patriotism; third, India now knows that she can depend on the Western powers to come to her aid, whereas the Russian reaction is still uncertain. India's future relations with each of the Himalayan kingdoms will be affected strongly by these facts. Already, in the case of Bhutan, India has given in to a degree on participation in international organizations such as the Colombo Plan. Conversely, it is possible that India may adopt a harder line toward Nepal, even to the point of taking positive, physical action. There are some parallels to the United States-Cuban relationship here.

Gandhi once wrote, "Brute force has been the ruling factor in the world for thousands of years; there is little hope of anything good coming out of it in future." It is ironic but perhaps inevitable that the huge country which attained independence through Gandhian non-violence should have to defend its Himalayan borderlands by military association with the West. Whether anything good will come out of it remains to be seen, but India has eagerly chosen it as the only course open to her to escape a much worse fate.

Appendix

The Himalayan Kingdoms—Area, Population, Political Status, and Resources

	Nepal	Sikkim	Bhutan
Area (in square miles)	54,563	2,828	18,000
Population	9,500,000 (1962 estimate)	167,000 (1961 census)	850,000 (1963 estimate)
Approximate Density per square mile	174	59	47
Political Status	Kingdom, joined U.N. 1955	Kingdom, protectorate of India	Kingdom, foreign affairs and defense guided by India
Capital	Katmandu, linked with India by air and modern highway	Gangtok, linked by modern highway with India	Thimbu, not easily accessible; motorable road link with India completed in 1963.
Government	Direct royal rule, elected government dismissed 1960	King assisted by an elected State Council	King assisted by an elected Advisory Assembly (Tsongdu)
Agricultural Products	A. Rice, sugarcane, jute in Terai.	A. Rice in lower valleys	A. Rice in lower valleys
	B. Rice and wheat in Inner Himalayan valleys	B. Rice and subtropical crops in Inner Himalayan valleys	B. Rice and subtropical crops in Inner Himalayan valleys
	C. Barley, potatoes in higher valleys of Great Himalaya	C. Barley, potatoes and hardy crops at higher elevations	C. Barley, potatoes and hardy crops at higher elevations
Mineral and Other Resources	Insignificant mineral resources, timber	Rich copper mines, timber	Mineral deposits unknown, timber

A Generalized Chart of the Himalayan Ecology in Nepal, Sikkim, and Bhutan

Elevation in feet	Climate	Economy		Settlements	Culture
		Agriculture	*Pastoralism*		
15,000 –	Ice Cap EF*			Snow Line	
12,000 –	Subarctic Dwc, Dwd (in some areas, BS)	Oat for fodder, Potatoes	Yak, Sheep Transhumance	Agglomerated Gable or Flat Roof Stone Houses	Pure Tibetan descent, Lamaistic Buddhism, Tibeto-Burman languages
9,000 –		Wheat and Barley; one crop per year	Yak, Sheep, Goat Transhumance		
6,000 –	Temperate Cwb	Barley and Wheat in winter, buckwheat in summer; two crops per year	Cattle, Goat, Donkey Transhumance; Buffalo	Dispersed settlements (stone wall, thatched, hipped roof)	Zone of mixture (complex interplay of Tibetan kinship and Indian penetration)
3,000 –	Warm Temperate Cwa	Maize, African millet; rice recessive	Buffalo, Indian Cattle		
500 –	Subtropical Cwa	Rice dominant	Buffalo, Indian Cattle	Mainly compact mud walls, tiled or thatched ridge-roof	Indian descent, Hinduism, Indo-Aryan languages
0 –					

* The letter symbols represent various climatic types in the Köppen classification of climates. Each letter has a specific definition in exact temperature or amount of precipitation. Thus, a mild-winter, moist-summer climate with long, hot summers is called Cwa. If the summers are warm rather than hot, it is known as Cwb. BS refers to a semi-arid, cold climate. Dwc stands for a severe-winter, moist-summer climate with very short, cool summers. If the winters are excessively cold, the climate is known as Dwd. EF refers to the polar climate, or icecap, in which plant growth is impossible.

Bibliography

BOOKS

Bowles, C., *Ambassador's Report,* Harper, New York, 1954, pp. 261-295.

Datar, B. N., *Himalayan Pilgrimage,* Publications Division, Govt. of India, Delhi, 1961.

Hagen, Toni, *Nepal: The Kingdom in the Himalaya,* Kummerly Frey, Berne, 1961.

Iijma, Shigeru, *Agriculture and Land System in Nepal,* Tokyo, 1961.

Jain, Girilal, *India Meets China in Nepal,* Asia Publishing House, Bombay and New York, 1959.

Karan, Pradyumna P., in collaboration with William M. Jenkins, *Nepal: A Cultural and Physical Geography,* University of Kentucky Press, Lexington, Ky., 1960. (Contains an authoritative list of more than 200 bibliographical items)

Snellgrove, David, *Himalayan Pilgrimage,* Bruno Cassirer, Oxford, 1961.

ARTICLES

Armstrong, Hamilton Fish, "Where India Faces China," *Foreign Affairs,* Vol. 37, July, 1959, pp. 617-625.

Doig, Desmond, "Sikkim, Tiny Himalayan Kingdom in the Clouds," *National Geographic Magazine,* Vol. 123, March, 1963, pp. 398-429.

Doig, Desmond, "Bhutan, the Mountain Kingdom," *National Geographic Magazine,* Vol. 120, Sept., 1961, pp. 384-415.

Hagen, Toni, "Afoot in Roadless Nepal," *National Geographic Magazine,* Vol. 117, 1960, pp. 361-405.

Karan, P. P., "Bhutan and Sikkim: Himalayan Shangri-La, Now Darkened by Communist China's Shadow, Faces Up to the 20th Century," *Canadian Geographical Journal,* Vol. 65, Dec., 1962, pp. 200-209.

Karan, P. P., and Alice Taylor, "Nepal," *Focus,* American Geographical Society, New York. Revised and reprinted Dec., 1961.

Palmer, Norman D., "Trans-Himalayan Confrontation," *Orbis,* Vol. 6, Winter, 1963, pp. 513-527.

Pant, Y. P., "Growth of Population in Nepal," *Eastern World,* Vol. 16, Sept., 1962, pp. 11-12.

Index